CULTURE SMART!

GEORGIA

Natia Abramia

·K·U·P·E·R·A·R·D·

ISBN 978 1 85733 654 2
This book is also available as an e-book: eISBN 978 1 85733 658 0

British Library Cataloguing in Publication Data
A CIP catalogue entry for this book is available from the British Library

First published in Great Britain
by Kuperard, an imprint of Bravo Ltd
59 Hutton Grove, London N12 8DS
Tel: +44 (0) 20 8446 2440   Fax: +44 (0) 20 8446 2441
www.culturesmart.co.uk
Inquiries: sales@kuperard.co.uk

Distributed in the United States and Canada
by Random House Distribution Services
1745 Broadway, New York, NY 10019
Tel: +1 (212) 572-2844   Fax: +1 (212) 572-4961
Inquiries: csorders@randomhouse.com

Series Editor Geoffrey Chesler
Design Bobby Birchall

Printed in Malaysia

About the Author

NATIA ABRAMIA is a Georgian journalist based in London. Before joining the BBC she worked in Tbilisi as a TV host and reporter covering news and current affairs. She also taught Conflict Reporting at the Georgian Institute of Public Affairs, and worked as an interpreter for high-profile negotiations and top-level meetings. After completing an MA in International Journalism at Cardiff University, Natia went on to produce TV documentaries, including films on the Balkans and Kashmir, an interview with the Dalai Lama, and features on multiculturalism and diversity. Currently she trains journalists in multiplatform production and works as a producer on flagship programs at the BBC World Service.

**The Culture Smart! series is continuing to expand.
For further information and latest titles visit
www.culturesmart.co.uk**

The publishers would like to thank **CultureSmart!**Consulting for its help in researching and developing the concept for this series.

CultureSmart!Consulting creates tailor-made seminars and consultancy programs to meet a wide range of corporate, public-sector, and individual needs. Whether delivering courses on multicultural team building in the USA, preparing Chinese engineers for a posting in Europe, training call-center staff in India, or raising the awareness of police forces to the needs of diverse ethnic communities, it provides essential, practical, and powerful skills worldwide to an increasingly international workforce.

For details, visit www.culturesmartconsulting.com

CultureSmart!Consulting and **CultureSmart!** guides have both contributed to and featured regularly in the weekly travel program "Fast Track" on BBC World TV.

contents

About the Author

NATIA ABRAMIA is a Georgian journalist based in London. Before joining the BBC she worked in Tbilisi as a TV host and reporter covering news and current affairs. She also taught Conflict Reporting at the Georgian Institute of Public Affairs, and worked as an interpreter for high-profile negotiations and top-level meetings. After completing an MA in International Journalism at Cardiff University, Natia went on to produce TV documentaries, including films on the Balkans and Kashmir, an interview with the Dalai Lama, and features on multiculturalism and diversity. Currently she trains journalists in multiplatform production and works as a producer on flagship programs at the BBC World Service.

contents

contents

Map of Georgia

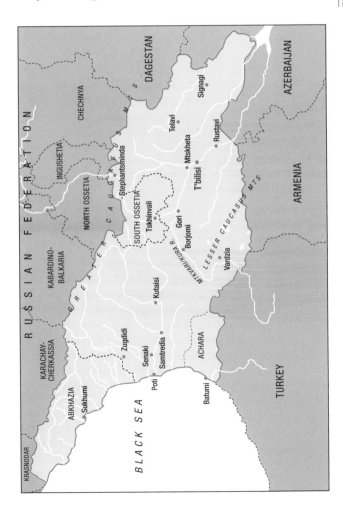

introduction

Georgia lies between Eastern Europe, Central
Asia, and the Middle East, on the southeastern
shore of the Black Sea. This small Caucasian
country is used to playing a significant role in
global geopolitics, though its strategic location
at the crossroads of different civilizations has been
a curse as well as a blessing. Once a battlefield of
the Christian and Muslim worlds, today it is
caught between its NATO aspirations and its
location in Russia's backyard.

The Silk Road, the great overland trade route
between Europe and China, brought the world to
Georgia. Its ancient Christian culture reflects the
contributions of Arab, Persian, and Ottoman
conquerors. Combined with this is a southern,
"Mediterranean" feel, traces of the old Soviet
legacy, and a very pronounced modern Western
influence. What awaits the visitor is a unique
culture dating back thousands of years. As well as
this rich heritage, Georgia offers wonderful food
and wines, unforgettable scenery, authentic folk
music and dances, an attractive business climate,
and an educated and hospitable people for whom
indulging a guest is more a religion than a duty.

Culture Smart! Georgia sets out to provide
insights and practical tips for tourists and
businesspeople alike. It will guide you through the
complex realities of the country, explaining what
motivates people, how they live and feel—and
how to relate to them.

Writing this book about my homeland has been an eye-opening experience. I discovered that some "facts" about Georgia's past and present were just perceptions or desires. More than ever, though, I have come to appreciate how special Georgians are. Cousins, friends, former colleagues and neighbors, just acquaintances, or people I had never met, wrote to give me advice, provide interesting quotes, or made phone calls to check information for me. Some have contributed to this book—you will see their names inside. There are also many others who are not mentioned and who have helped with the usual Georgian kindness and natural warmth. It is impossible to give all their names. I can only thank them—*Madloba*.

Visitors may find Georgians impulsive, macho, hotheaded, short-termist, obstinate, and poor timekeepers—but they are also warm, proud, generous, expressive, loyal, clever, flexible, and traditional yet stylish. My overseas respondents who have traveled to Georgia have helped me to understand how foreigners see the country. I have interviewed dozens of Westerners who have visited Tbilisi and the regions as tourists or for business. Their input has been invaluable. All of them have brought their views and their stories to the book. Most of them were unanimous about one thing: Georgia is a place to visit and Georgians are people to be friends with; if you touch their hearts, they will charm you back.

Key Facts

Official Name	Georgia	In Georgian, Sakartvelo ("Land of Georgians")
Capital	Tbilisi	Population 1.1 million (2010 Census)
Major Cities	Kutaisi, Batumi, Poti, Zugdidi, Gori, Telavi	Sokhumi, Gagra, and Ckhinvali are currently in conflict zones.
Area	26,911 square miles (69,700 sq. km)	Approximately 20% of its total territory is not under Georgian government control.
Borders	To the south, Turkey, Armenia, and Azerbaijan. To the north, Russia and the federal subject republics of Karachay-Cherkessia, Kabardino-Balkaria, North Ossetia, Ingushetia, Chechnya, and Dagestan	
Climate	Generally moderate; mild on the Black Sea coast with cold winters in the mountains.	January is the coldest month, July the hottest, and May the wettest.
Currency	1 Georgian Lari (GEL) = 100 tetri	
Population	4.6 million	
Ethnic Makeup	Georgian 83.8%, Azeri 6.5%, Armenian 5.7%, Russian 1.5%, other 2.5%. (2011 est.)	

Language	Georgian 71% (official), Russian 9%, Armenian 7%, Azeri 6%, other 7%	Abkhaz and Ossetian are "official languages" in the Autonomous Republic of Abkhazia and South Ossetia.
Religion	Orthodox Christian 83.9%, Muslim 9.9%, Armenian Apostolic 3.9%, Catholic 0.8%; other 0.8%; none 0.7%	
Government	Multiparty democracy. Unicameral parliament of 235 seats; members serve 4-year terms.	The head of state is the President, elected every 5 years. Eligible for 2 terms
Media	More than 140 media outlets. National TV channnels: GPB (Georgian public broadcaster). Rustavi2 and Imedi are major private netwoks. All three TV channels are controlled by the government.	Newspapers: *Kviris palitra*, *Rezonanasi*, *24 Saati*. Main English-language newspapers: *The Financial*, *The Georgian Times*, *The Georgian Journal*, and *The Messenger*.
Electricity	220 volts, 50 Hz	Plugs have two round prongs
Video/TV	PAL/SECAM	
Internet Domain	.ge	
Telephone	The country code for Georgia is 995.	
Time Zone	UTC/GMT + 4 hours	No daylight saving in 2012

chapter one

LAND &
PEOPLE

GEOGRAPHY

Georgia is situated at the junction of Eastern Europe and Western Asia in the region known as the Caucasus—Caucasia, as the locals call it. It shares borders with the Russian republics of Chechnya, Ingushetia, and North Ossetia to the north and northeast, with Azerbaijan, Armenia, and Turkey to the south. The shoreline of the Black Sea forms its western border.

With an area of 26,216 sq. miles (67,900 sq. km), Georgia has a dramatic and varied landscape,

encompassing snowcapped mountains, valleys, glaciers, gorges, volcanic plateaus, hot springs, lakes, forests, subtropical wetlands on the coast, and semidesert plains in the southeast. It ranks among the world's top twelve countries for geographical diversity.

The northern border is formed by the Greater Caucasus mountain range, and the southern border by the Lesser Caucasus mountains. The Greater Caucasus is the higher of the two, with peaks rising to more than 16,404 feet (5,000 m) above sea level.

Georgia has about 25,000 rivers, flowing westward into the Black Sea and eastward through Azerbaijan to the Caspian Sea. The most important river is the Mtkvari (also known by its Turkish name, Kura), which flows 847 miles (1,364 km) from northeast Turkey across the plains of eastern Georgia, through the capital Tbilisi and into the Caspian Sea.

Thanks to a benevolent climate and fertile soil, agriculture has always been important to Georgia. There are about a thousand mineral springs, the best known of which are the springs at Borjomi. For millennia Georgia has been famous for wine making, and today it produces hundreds of different wines. The Georgians have a creation story explaining how they came to be so blessed (see box overleaf).

If you should hear this story in Georgia, it will be told with some humor and a lot of pride: Georgians truly believe that they are chosen and that they got extremely lucky with their homeland. Compare this account to "God created the world, but the Dutch created the Netherlands" and make your own judgment of the national character.

HOW THE GEORGIANS GAINED THEIR PARADISE ON EARTH

There was a time when there were no borders, no countries or cities, and people just lived together. Then at some point God decided to distribute the land among the people and let them build their own states. At first, the Georgians did not receive anything—they were having a party and arrived late for the meeting with the Creator. One Georgian (pretty drunk, but still able to manage his manners) approached God and apologized sincerely.

"Sorry, Lord," he said, "please excuse us and give us a little piece of land; we don't need an awful lot."

"There is nothing left," said God, "I have now given away everything on this planet."

"Well, I have to be honest here, Lord," said the man, "We were drinking and we could not have stopped halfway through. We had raised a glass to you, then everyone had to toast and praise you in turn . . . . it takes time. You know that."

God knew what Georgians were like and was not very surprised, so he gave them what he had intended to keep for himself and then ascended to Heaven.

CLIMATE

Georgia's temperature varies widely because of its diverse landscape, but in general the country has all four seasons: summers are very hot; fall is warm and sunny; winters are white, and give way quickly to exhilarating springs. If you like the idea of living in a sunny country with breathtaking fall foliage and an occasional snowfall, this is the place to be.

The climate is moderated by the Greater Caucasus mountain range, which serves as a barrier against cold air from Siberia. The climatic zones are determined by their distance from the Black Sea and by altitude; warm, moist air spreads inland from the Black Sea.

Tbilisi is moderately humid and subtropical, with relatively cold winters and hot summers: January is the coldest month, July the hottest, and May the wettest. An average January temperature is 33.6°F (0.9°C). In July it reaches 75.9°F (24.4°C). The absolute minimum recorded temperature is −9°F (−23°C) and the absolute maximum is 104°F (40°C). Snow falls on average 15 to 25 days a year. Tbilisi is beautiful when it's wrapped in white.

In west Georgia, the climate is subtropical up to about 2,133 ft (650 m); above that altitude (and to the north and east) is a band of moist and moderately warm weather, then a band of cool and

wet conditions. In the eastern part of the country summer temperatures average 68°F (20°C) to 75.2°F (24°C), winter temperatures 35.6°F (2°C) to 39.2°F (4°C). Humidity is lower, and rainfall averages 19.7 to 31.5 in (500 to 800 mm) a year.

All over the country March is the only month with totally unpredictable weather: it might be sunny in the morning, windy in the afternoon, and rainy in the evening. So, when describing impulsive characters, Georgians often say that they are like the sky in March.

THE PEOPLE

According to the National Statistics Office of Georgia, in 2011 the population of the country was 4,469,200, out of which 1,162,400 lived in Tbilisi.

GEORGIAN ETHNIC GROUPS (2011)
Georgians 3,661,173
Azerbaijanis 284,761
Armenians 248,929
Russians 67,671
Ossetians 38,028
Yezids 18,329
Greeks 15,166
Kists (ethnic group related to Chechens) 7,110
Ukrainians 7,039
Abkhazians 3,527

Genetic studies classify Georgians as Caucasoid. The country's main genetic group is one that is also found in Greece and Italy.

Religion

According to the 2002 census, 83.8 percent of
the population are Georgian Orthodox. Fewer
than 10 percent are Muslim; because of Persian
influence East Georgian Muslims are Shias,
mainly Azerbaijani and North
Caucasian ethnic communities.
West Georgian Muslims on the
Black Sea coast are Sunni and
are strongly linked with Turkey.
The Armenian Apostolic
Church accounts for
3.9 percent, most of whom
are ethnic Armenians living
near the border with Armenia,
where they constitute the
majority of the local
population.

Jews have lived in Georgia
since ancient times, and a number of Jewish
communities still exist across the country. After
two major waves of emigration, in the 1970s and
late 1980s, only one-twelfth of the country's
previous Jewish population—around eight
thousand individuals—remain in Georgia.

Regions and Subcultures

Georgia is divided into nine regions, one city, and
three autonomous republics, two of which are not
under the control of Tbilisi. The natural barriers
presented by the Lesser Caucasus mountain range
have had a strong influence on the cultural and
linguistic differences between the Georgian regions.
History has also played its part in fostering diversity
between subgroups. After the medieval period

Georgia broke up into several states that were often at war with one another.

The process of nation formation has been a complex one, and the Georgian people today comprise a colorful set of subgroups, each with its own characteristic traditions, manners, dialect, and, in the case of Mingrelians and Svans, their own language.

How To Tell Who's Who

Family names in the mountainous Georgian provinces can be distinguished by the suffixes –uri, -uli, or -ani. Mingrelians have last names ending in -ia, -ua, or -va. So we can tell from their family names that Stalin's henchman Beria and the NBA's Zaza Pachulia have Mingrelian roots. The most common endings are -shvili ("child of") and -ze ("son of"), as in Saakashvili and Shevardnadze, however. Both are found all over the country, especially in the regions of Kartli, Guria, Imereti, and Kakheti.

Because of the high elevation and poor roads, the mountainous regions of Svaneti, Mtiuleti, and Khevi are virtually cut off from the outside world during the long winters. The villagers there are ascribed particular characteristics, and are often the butt of jokes by other Georgians. People say, for example, that if a Svan's feet hurt because his shoes are too small, he'll think that what he needs is a painkiller. Another joke is that Svans will keep their computer mouse locked away so the cat doesn't eat it.

People in eastern and central Georgia are said to be thoughtful, direct, quiet, and earnest, but a little dim-witted; they've somehow earned the reputation of being slow on the uptake. Western Georgians—Imeretians, Gurians, Mingrelians, and Ajarians—on the other hand, are considered to be more lighthearted and to have a better sense of humor—with the caveat that they might not be as open and honest as their eastern brothers. Such perceptions have never been evaluated objectively, but there are hundreds of jokes and anecdotes about these differences, which Georgians like to tell to their guests and to each other.

TBILISI—A CITY OF WARMTH

Sir Fitzroy MacLean, the Scottish soldier, writer, and diplomat who was posted to the British Embassy in Moscow in the 1930s, made many unauthorized journeys to the eastern USSR. It has been speculated that he was one of Ian Fleming's inspirations for James Bond. This is how he described Tbilisi in his 1949 book *Eastern Approaches*. Back then it was known as Tiflis:

"Tiflis . . . has a graceful quality, a southern charm, an air of leisure, which I had so far found nowhere else in the Soviet Union. In the old city the houses, crazy structures with jutting verandas, hang like swallows' nests from the side of a hill. Beneath them a mountain stream tumbles its rushing waters and more houses cluster on the far side. Where the valley opens out a broad avenue leads to the newer part of the town, built by the Russians after the conquest of Georgia a century ago . . . . Half of the charm of Tiflis lies in its people. They are southerners and wine drinkers, mountaineers and fighters. They combine a truly Mediterranean expansiveness and vivacity with the dash and hardiness of the Highlander. As a race, they are strikingly good-looking: the men dark, wiry and aggressive in their long cloaks and sheepskin hats on the side of their heads; the women high-breasted and dark-eyed, with straight classical features. Racially they are neither Slavs, like the Russians, nor Turks, like the Tartars, but belong to a race of their own with its own ancient language and customs."

Situated on the banks of the Mtkvari (Kura) River, Tbilisi occupied a strategic position at the crossroads of important Silk Road trade routes, and has been influenced by many rival powers and empires. It has been destroyed and rebuilt around twenty-nine times, and the city's history is apparent in its architecture. Central Tbilisi is a mixture of different styles, including the narrow streets of the medieval Kala district, the ruins of the Narika fortress guarding the city, the ancient Turkish baths, and Paris/Hausmann-inspired Rustaveli Avenue featuring the Moorish-style Opera House.

The urban architecture also carries strong reminders of the Soviet era, with modern housing developments alongside the massive buildings of the "Stalin period" and identical blocks of "Khrushchev apartments" that were built quickly and cheaply for Soviet families.

THE LEGEND OF TBILISI

At the beginning of the fifth century, King Vakhtang Gorgasali accidentally discovered hot springs while hunting in the environs of Tbilisi. His falcon caught a pheasant, but soon both disappeared. After some time the king's hunting dogs found the birds—both had fallen into a warm sulfur spring and were boiled. King Vakhtang decided to build a new capital on the spot and to call it Tbilisi, as *tbili* means "warm" in Georgian. So Tbilisi was founded in the fifth century, but the capital was moved there from Mtskheta only in the next century.

A BRIEF HISTORY

The Georgians call themselves Kartvelebi, and their land Sakartvelo. These names are derived from a mythical king, Kartlos, said to be the father of all Georgians. According to the Georgian Chronicles Kartlos was the great-grandson of the biblical Japhet, one of Noah's sons. The name Georgia, used throughout Western Europe, is mistakenly believed to come from the country's patron saint, St. George.

The country actually got its foreign name from the Greeks, who were impressed by the way the Georgians worked the land (earth is *geo* in Greek). Other names for Georgia are Gurj in Turkish and Gruzin in Slavic languages.

The first Georgian state, the kingdom of Colchis, came into being in the eleventh century BCE, along the eastern shores of the Black Sea. Colchis civilization flourished with the development of smelting and metal casting. Sophisticated farming implements were developed and the fertile, well-watered lowlands and mild climate contributed to the growth of advanced agricultural techniques. In the sixth and fifth centuries BCE the ancient Greeks established trading cities on the Black Sea coast. In time the kingdom of Colchis disintegrated, but a successor kingdom known as Egrisi continued until the seventh century CE.

MEDEA

The ancient myth of the Argonauts tells the story of the band of fifty Greek demigods and heroes led by Jason, who, in order to win back his rightful place on the throne of Iolus, sailed to Colchis in his quest for the Golden Fleece.

Medea, daughter of King Aeetes of Colchis and granddaughter of the sun god Helios, fell in love with Jason and promised to help him, on the condition that if he succeeded he would marry her and take her with him. Jason agreed, and the princess, who was a healer and knew about secret herbal medicines (the word "medicine" could have been derived from her name), gave him some ointment. Empowered by this miraculous substance, Jason managed to overcome all the challenges (fighting flame-breathing bulls and drawing and sowing the teeth of a dragon), steal the Fleece, and sail to Greece with Medea. The Greek tragedy, written by Euripides in 431 BCE, depicts Medea as a disappointed and jealous wife who is unable to find her place after eloping to Greece. When Jason betrays her, she takes revenge for his adultery by killing their two sons.

Georgians think that the tale of Medea's revenge was invented by Euripides. They believe, however, that the story accurately reflects certain aspects of life in the ancient kingdom of Colchis. Even today ointments and herbal remedies are produced in west Georgia. Some family recipes for painkillers and anti-inflammatory balms for burns, bruises, and cuts pass down from one generation to another. So Georgians believe that their ancestors had a long tradition of producing herbal remedies, with some of the secret recipes dating back to antiquity.

Georgian geologists have found firm evidence that sheepskin was used in gold mining in the country's mountain rivers. It is possible that the Golden Fleece was a symbol of secret ancient mining techniques rather than a physical object. The natives mine gold from the rivers even in modern day Svaneti. So the ancient myth of the Argonauts definitely contains an element of truth.

Shortly before Colchis disintegrated, the kingdom of Kartli (known as Iberia to classical writers), was established in east Georgia with its capital in Mtskheta. Kartli and Colchis shared a common fate under Roman and Persian invaders. The history of Kartli would be dominated by the power struggle between the neighboring empires.

The first king of Kartli was Parnavaz I, whose story is saturated with legendary imagery and symbolism. According to medieval sources, this model pre-Christian monarch ruled in the third century BCE. His paternal uncle was a leader of the Georgian tribes around Mtskheta; it is believed that his mother was Iranian. The story of Parnavaz, although written by a Christian chronicler, is reminiscent of an ancient Iranian myth. The young Parnavaz's family was destroyed and his inheritance usurped by Azon, according to various sources a local ruler's son who was installed as king of Kartli by Alexander the Great during his campaign there (which the Greek historians did not, however, record).

Parnavaz was brought up fatherless, but was encouraged to undertake heroic deeds by a magical dream, in which he anointed himself with the essence of the sun. He then set off and went hunting. In pursuit of a deer, he came across a mass of treasure stored in a hidden cave. Parnavaz retrieved the treasure and used it to raise a loyal army against the tyrannical Azon. He was aided by Kuji, lord of Egrisi (previously Colchis), who eventually married Parnavaz's sister. Azon was defeated and killed, and Parnavaz became king of Kartli at the age of twenty-seven. He supervised the erection in Mtskheta of the idol of Armazi (supreme deity in the pre-Christian Georgian pantheon), and the construction of a similarly named fortress. He is also alleged to have invented the Georgian alphabet.

The Coming of Christianity
In the fourth century Christianity became the state religion of the kingdom of Kartli, at that time ruled by King Mirian III.

St. Nino and the Royal Conversions
According to legend, when St. Nino arrived in Georgia in c. 320 she found the people worshiping idols. Mirian's wife, Queen Nana, was ill: she was dying and no one could help her. Only after St. Nino prayed for her did she recover and declare a wish to be baptized a Christian. Neither King Mirian nor the Georgian people wanted to give up their pagan religion, but this changed after an incident during the royal hunt.

One day, when the king was hunting in dense woodland near Mtskheta, it suddenly grew dark and he lost his way. Terrified, he began praying to his idols, to no avail. In desperation he prayed to St. Nino's god—Jesus Christ—and the sun reappeared and he was able to see. After this miracle Mirian converted and made Christianity the state religion. Shortly afterward, the west Georgian kingdom of Colchis also adopted the Christian faith.

Today it is generally thought that Christianity was declared the official religion in Georgia before 337. Some historians argue that what the king experienced was a total solar eclipse on the evening of May 6, 319.

With the adoption of Christianity, Kartli and Egrisi forged political ties with the Eastern Roman (later the Byzantine) Empire, which exerted a strong cultural influence over them. The kingdom of Kartli, however, fell under Persian control for long periods throughout the fifth century.

IBERIA AND IBERIA

"Since the time of Plato and Aristotle, writers and scientists have referred in various manuscripts to two 'Iberias.' Before our era, it was common for travelers to call Spain 'Western Iberia' and Kartli 'Eastern Iberia.'

It is possible that Iberians from the Caucasus emigrated to the Pyrenees and settled in modern day Spain millennia ago—or the other way round. It is also possible that Iberian civilization flourished around the Mediterranean; it stretched from the Pyrenees as far as the Caucasus until various Indo-European groups moved in and settled the area. The Iberians were assimilated, but their traces can still be found in Corsica, Sardinia, and the Basque country. The Spanish called their country Iberia until the third century AD. The Georgians maintained the name and statehood until the Russian annexation of the nineteenth century. Traces of this old civilization can be seen in the ethno-culture and traditions of these two peoples, but they are buried under so many layers of history that it is hard to get to the root and find the evidence to prove the associated theories.

Some of the similarities are obvious—just listen to Georgian and Basque or Corsican polychromic music and the polyphonic (many-voiced) folk songs to make your own judgment. There are numerous parallels and homonyms in the languages of the people whose countries once shared the name Iberia. These similarities, especially the place names, along with parallel traditional games and festivals, still have to be studied. The biggest discovery is yet to be made."

Dato Turashvili, Georgian author

According to Donald Rayfield, professor of Russian and Georgian at the University of London, before the tenth century Georgian history is composed of legends, myths, and stories that are possible but not probable.

In the tenth century Bagrat III (978–1014) gradually united the Georgian kingdoms and lands, becoming the first king of Qartvelta Samefo—the Kingdom of Georgians. The Bagrationi dynasty, said to have descended from the biblical King David, ruled continuously until the end of the eighteenth century, when the Russian Empire dethroned the heir. They were the longest ruling dynasty in Europe.

By the late seventh century, Byzantine–Persian rivalry for control of the Middle East had given way to the Arab conquest of the region. In the second half of the eleventh century, Arab invaders and Seljuq Turks devastated most of Georgia, to such an extent that by the end of the 1080s they outnumbered Georgians there.

David Agmashenebeli (1073–1125) led the struggle against the Seljuq invaders. The sixteen-year-old heir of the Bagrationi royal family acceded to the throne in 1089. After a successful military campaign he liberated most of the Georgian lands apart from the capital, Tbilisi. In 1121, the Seljuq Sultan Mahmud declared *jihad* on

Georgia and sent a large army to fight the Georgians. Although significantly outnumbered by the Turks, the Georgians managed to defeat them at the Battle of Didgori, and took Tbilisi—the last remaining Muslim enclave in the area formerly under Arab occupation. "David the Builder" ushered in a reign of enlightened religious tolerance and established institutions of learning.

His successors continued the policy of expansion by subordinating most of the mountain clans and tribes of the North Caucasus.

David's great-granddaughter, Queen Tamar (1160–1213), was the most glorious sovereign of medieval Georgia. First co-regent

with her father, and then ruler in her own right, she created a strong feudal monarchy that controlled a great pan-Caucasian empire. Her era is considered the golden age of Georgian history, marked by political and military achievements and the development of culture, architecture, literature, philosophy, and sciences.

VEFXISTKAOSANI—GEORGIA'S NATIONAL EPIC

> By shedding tears of blood we praise King
> [i.e. Queen] Tamara, whose praises I
> have told forth.
> For ink I have used a lake of jet, and for
> pen a pliant crystal.
> Whoever hears, a jagged spear will pierce
> his heart!

With these words the medieval poet Shota Rustaveli dedicated his epic *Vefxistkaosani* (The Knight in the Panther's Skin) to Queen Tamar. It is not known if he was really in love with her or whether this expression of devotion was simply a convention of the age, but the epic poem is a source of pride for Georgians. Written between 1196 and 1207, it celebrates chivalry, love, friendship, courage, and fortitude.

The Mongols invaded Georgia in the 1220s, along with the South Caucasus and Asia Minor. Georgian King George V "the Brilliant" expelled them, united the country, and converted the pagans of the mountain regions to Christianity. In the later fourteenth century the Islamic Turko-Mongol conqueror of Asia, Tamerlane (Timūr-e Lang, or Timur the Lame) raided Georgia on eight occasions, devastating the economy, slaughtering the population, and sacking its cities. Although Tamerlane was not able to defeat the Georgians decisively, he dealt the country a crippling blow. By the middle of the fifteenth century, most of Georgia's old neighbor-states had disappeared from the map. The fall of Constantinople to the Ottoman Turks in 1453 isolated the Georgians from the rest of the Christian world.

From the sixteenth century the Ottoman Empire and a new Muslim power, Safavid Persia, divided the Georgian lands between themselves. In the next few hundred years Georgia would become a battleground for these rival powers. The west fell to the Turks and the east to the Persians. Tens of thousands of Georgians were killed or deported to Persia by the Safavid ruler, Shah Abbas.

The Russian Empire
By the seventeenth century, as the result of constant warfare,

both east and west Georgia had sunk into poverty. Erekle II (1720–98), king of East Georgia, or Kartl-Kakheti, turned to Russia and in 1783 signed the Treaty of Georgievsk, according to which Kartl-Kakheti would receive Russian protection against Ottoman and Persian attacks. But the Russians soon withdrew their troops from the region for use elsewhere. In 1795, the Persian Shah, Agha Mohammad Khan, invaded the country and razed the capital, Tbilisi, to the ground.

The Georgian rulers still felt they had nobody else to turn to, and in 1789 the ailing King George XII sent envoys to ask Russia for protection once again. In the midst of negotiations, however, in 1801, Tsar Paul I of Russia signed a decree unilaterally incorporating East Georgia into the Russian Empire, abolishing the Bagrationi dynasty and the independence of the Georgian Orthodox Church.

In 1810, the west Georgian kingdom of Imereti was annexed by Tsar Alexander I. As a result of numerous Russian wars against Turkey and Persia, several formerly independent Georgian territories were occupied by the Russians. So Georgia was reunified for the first time in centuries, but had lost its liberty.

The Democratic Republic of Georgia, 1918–21
The Revolution of October 1917 plunged Russia into a bloody civil war during which several outlying Russian territories declared independence. Georgia proclaimed the establishment of the

independent Democratic Republic of Georgia (DRG) on May 26, 1918. Parliamentary elections were won by the Georgian Social-Democratic Party. Though Georgia was recognized by Soviet Russia as well as the major Western powers, the Red Army invaded Georgia in 1921 and occupied the country after a short war. The elected government was forced to flee abroad.

Soviet rule was consolidated after the Red Army and Cheka (security police) forces under Joseph Stalin and Sergo Ordzhonikidze crushed an anti-Bolshevik uprising in 1924. Georgia was incorporated into the Transcaucasian Socialist Federative Soviet Republic (TSFSR), which consisted of Georgia, Armenia, and Azerbaijan. In 1936 the TSFSR was dissolved and split into the Georgian, Armenian, and Azerbaijan Soviet Socialist Republics (SSRs).

Georgia under the Soviet Union, 1921–90

Stalin rose to the highest position in the Soviet Union, and millions would lose their lives under his rule. He systematically eliminated his rivals and created a totalitarian police state that enforced rapid industrialization, the collectivization of agriculture, and a centralized economy. Stalin created a cult of personality that elevated him to near godlike status.

"Stalin's Ass"

In his book *Young Stalin*, Simon Sebag Montefiore suggests that the status of Georgia triggered Stalin's schism with Lenin:

"The Old Man was content to leave Georgia, but in 1921 Stalin and Sergo Ordzhonikidze arranged a successful invasion. The dashing, merciless Sergo rode triumphantly into Tiflis on a white horse, but he soon earned the nickname 'Stalin's Ass' for his brutal suppression of the country. When it came to defining the status of Georgia, Stalin insisted that it join a Transcaucasian Federation, but the local Bolsheviks . . . demanded a separate Georgian Republic. . . . Lenin now supported the Georgians against Stalin and Sergo. This led to Stalin's insulting Lenin's wife Krupskaya. Lenin wrote his Testament that demanded Stalin's removal from the General Secretaryship. But it was too late. Lenin suffered another stroke. Stalin survived."

It is not known exactly how many were arrested, tortured, and executed during the Great Purge of 1937, but it's clear that during a series of campaigns of mass political repression and persecution, the Georgian population suffered immensely. The Great Terror took the lives of writers, intellectuals, and artists who died in prisons or were executed in gulags (concentration camps) or prisons after being charged with treason.

The Second World War

The Georgians contributed greatly to the defense of the USSR in the Great Patriotic War (1941–45). Almost 700,000 fighters joined the Soviet Army, more than half of whom would never return. The Republic provided a vital source of textiles and munitions for the southern front line.

After the war Georgia enjoyed privileged status compared to other Soviet republics. While the official growth rate of the Georgian economy was among the lowest in the USSR, personal savings and rates of car and house ownership were the highest. Of all the SSRs, Georgia had the largest proportion of people with a university degree.

In the 1960s a movement for the restoration of Georgian independence started to gain ground. Its leaders, Merab Kostava and Zviad Gamsakhurdia, were persecuted and their activities suppressed.

In 1985 Eduard Shevardnadze, the First Secretary of the Georgian Soviet Republic, was promoted to work in the Kremlin. As Minister of Foreign Affairs (1985–91) Shevardnadze, together with Mikhail Gorbachev, started reforming the Soviet Union and played a key role in the détente that preceded the end of the Cold War. The two wanted to rebuild the USSR. The Georgians, however, wanted it to collapse. As soon as the relatively liberal policies of *Glasnost* and *Perestroika* ("openness" and "restructuring") were announced, Georgians went out into the streets to protest.

On April 9, 1989, an anti-Soviet demonstration in Tbilisi was bloodily dispersed by the Soviet Army. The death of twenty people in this brutal crackdown led to full-scale protests.

THE PROTEST GENERATION

In his book *The Closed Society and its Guards*, the Georgian philosopher Georgi Maisuradze remembers embarking on his studies at Tbilisi State University in September 1988.

"Our generation was born and grew up on the streets," he says. "The protest movement defined how we spoke, argued, and even thought . . . . On 21st September 1988 a new era started in Georgia—the era of permanent demonstration, an era that is still ongoing . . . I have the feeling that the time has stood still in Georgia, that it is still 1988. More than twenty years on we are still at that protest, which has turned into a never-ending feast."

The October 1990 elections to the National Assembly—the first multiparty elections in the USSR—saw the anticommunist Round Table–Free Georgia party win by a clear margin. The country declared independence from the Soviet Union on April 9, 1991, and the national symbols used by the DRG were reinstated.

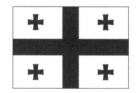

Post-Soviet Georgia

Zviad Gamsakhurdia, the leader of the independence movement, was elected president of Georgia in 1991. On taking office, he faced major economic and political difficulties. As the Soviet economy disintegrated, shortages became acute. After gaining their independence, Georgians found themselves spending long hours waiting in line for food. It was a period of confusion, and one in which people worried about how they would survive in this new environment.

In 1992 Gamsakhurdia was driven out of office in a bloody coup by elements of the National Guard and the Mikhedrion, a nationalist paramilitary organization.

The Silver Fox and the Rose Revolution
Nicknamed the "Silver Fox" for his gray hair and cunning diplomacy, in 1992 Eduard Shevardnadze was

brought in to join the leaders of the coup. In 1995 he was officially elected president. His rule would become associated with defeat in war, corruption, and weak governance. Famous in the West for bringing down the Berlin Wall, Shevardnadze was extremely unpopular in his own country. Following the collapse of the USSR, Georgia experienced a series of violent upheavals: the bloody

independence movement in April 1989, military operations in South Ossetia, armed clashes on the streets of Tbilisi as people sought to oust the country's first president, an unsuccessful war in Abkhazia, raids by Mkedrioni, groups of vigilantes, countless demonstrations, strikes, and protest marches.

In 2003 thousands of Georgians took to the streets once again. This time they were protesting the results of the November parliamentary elections, widely believed to have been rigged by the government. Demonstrations started in Tbilisi and spread across the country. When President Shevardnadze attempted to open the new session of parliament, supporters of the opposition parties led by Mikhail Saakashvili burst into the chamber with roses in their hands, interrupting his speech, and forcing him to escape with his bodyguards. On the evening of November 23 (St. George's Day in Georgia), Eduard Shevardnadze met with the opposition leaders and announced his resignation, prompting euphoria in the streets of Tbilisi. The Rose Revolution brought immense popularity to Mikhail Saakashvili, who was elected president of Georgia in 2004 with a 96 percent share of the vote.

The Rose Revolution raised many expectations, both at home and abroad. The new government was expected to bring democracy, ending a period of widespread corruption and inefficiency; and to complete state building by reasserting sovereignty over the whole of Georgia's territory. Most of these hopes were crushed, however, when Russia and Georgia went to war in August 2008.

NORTHERN NEIGHBOR, FROZEN CONFLICTS

At present Georgia is unable to control about 20 percent of its total area, which makes territorial integrity the country's prime problem. Official Tbilisi is adamant that there can be no compromise over the status of South Ossetia or Abkhazia. These former autonomous regions of Georgia are now recognized by Russia as independent states. Georgia sees this as a direct intervention in its internal affairs.

South Ossetia

During the twilight of the Soviet Union, violence erupted in the South Ossetian Autonomous Oblast within the Georgian Soviet Socialist Republic, between its independence-minded Georgian population and Ossetians loyal to the Soviet Union. After several outbreaks, the region declared its intention to secede from Georgia in 1990, and the following year declared de facto independence.

This led to the 1991–92 South Ossetian War, which ended in a standoff. In 2004 and 2008 there were renewed attempts by Georgia to gain control of the region. The 2008 Ossetian, or Russo-Georgian, War saw Russia openly allying itself with the separatists. In the course of the conflict Russian forces invaded west Georgia and occupied the cities of Poti, Gori, Senaki, and Zugdidi. Mediation by the EU resulted in a ceasefire and the Russians withdrew from Georgia proper, but Russian troops remain stationed in South Ossetia and Abkhazia.

Abkhazia

In August 1992, a separatist dispute in the Georgian Autonomous Republic of Abkhazia escalated into a full-scale war between Georgian forces and Abkhaz paramilitaries, assisted by Russia. In September 1993 the Georgians suffered a catastrophic defeat. Around 14,000 people died, and another 300,000 were forced to flee. Abkhazia declared independence from Georgia in 1999, and later, in 2008, joined the Ossetian fight against Georgia. Apart from by Russia and a handful of other countries, Abkhazia is not internationally recognized. Georgia continues to regard it as sovereign territory occupied by the Russian army.

These two disputed territories are the reason Georgia aspires to join NATO. At the same time these frozen conflicts are the very reason NATO is reluctant to accept it. That Georgia participates in NATO's Partnership for Peace program is the main pillar of disagreement with Russia, which still considers Georgia as its backyard and is keen to prevent a NATO presence reaching its borders.

POLITICAL LANDSCAPE AND DEMOCRACY

Georgia is a democratic, semi-presidential republic, with the President as the head of state, and the Prime Minister as the head of government.

In a recent survey, only 43 percent of Tbilisi residents said that they consider Georgia to be a democratic state. The number is higher in Kutaisi (49 percent) and Batumi (67 percent), and even higher in other towns and rural areas. The reason is that opposition TV stations are sometimes the only broadcasters reporting on undemocratic practices. Other surveys confirm that the rural population is more trusting of the media, more susceptible to media bias, and less informed about the real political situation. In rural areas people have more social problems, but they are still less critical of the current system and its leaders. In the capital, in contrast, as a result of greater awareness and political engagement, 37 percent of Tbilisi residents think that Georgia is governed by the rule of law, compared with 56 percent in rural areas. There seems to be confusion, however, about what the rule of law actually entails. When asked whether the government should act more as a parent toward the population or more as its servant, slightly under half the respondents said that the government should act as a parent.

Different opinions exist regarding the degree of political freedom in Georgia. President Saakashvili believes that the country is "on the road to becoming a European democracy." Freedom House, however, places Georgia in the group of partly free countries, along with states such as Ukraine, Bosnia and Herzegovina, and Macedonia.

THE ECONOMY

The political turmoil following Georgia's independence had a catastrophic effect on the country's economy. After the fall of the USSR in 1991, Georgia embarked on major structural reforms designed to transform it from a Soviet command economy to a free market economy. Like other post-Soviet states it faced severe economic collapse. The civil war and military conflicts in South Ossetia and Abkhazia aggravated the crisis. By the end of 1996 Georgia's economy had shrunk to around one-third of its size in 1989.

Today economic activity is based largely on agricultural products such as grapes, citrus fruits, and hazelnuts; the mining of manganese and copper; and a small industrial sector producing wine and beverages, metals, machinery, aircraft, and chemicals. Tourism is increasingly important. While the country imports nearly all its natural gas and oil supplies, hydropower is a growing energy resource. Georgia has renovated its hydropower plants and is increasingly switching to natural gas imported from Azerbaijan rather than from Russia.

The construction of oil and gas pipelines to Azerbaijan and Turkey, and a railroad to northern Turkey, are part of a strategy to capitalize on Georgia's location and develop its role as a transit point for gas, oil, and other goods between Europe and Asia.

Economic growth slowed down following the conflict with Russia in 2008. The Russian Federation was the major market to which Georgia had traditionally been linked. Growth indicators turned negative in 2009 when foreign direct investment and Georgian migrant workers' remittances declined in the wake of the global financial crisis. The economy bounced back in 2010–11, with growth rates above 5 percent per year, but foreign investment has not recovered fully and unemployment remains high.

Historically the collection of tax revenues has always been a problem in Georgia; however, the government has reduced the number of taxes and managed to improve tax administration; there has also been tremendous success in cracking down on petty corruption. As a result budget revenues have increased dramatically. There is a determined effort to continue to liberalize the economy by reducing regulation, taxes, and corruption in order to attract foreign investment.

More than 230,000 internally displaced persons have put an enormous strain on the economy. Official unemployment was 16.9 percent in 2010. On the positive side, though, the World Bank has recognized Georgia as one of the world's fastest-reforming economies and ranked it in the same tier as countries such as Australia, Norway, and Japan.

chapter two

VALUES & ATTITUDES

FREEDOM AND IDENTITY

"History defines individuals and nations; no one has ever been able to step away from their past. Our background—not just historical facts and events—shapes our values, traditions and beliefs. Our ancestors have fought for independence and have died to preserve their identity and the right to define their future. Why? Because freedom has become the central axis of identity for a Georgian man. A Georgian sees no valuable existence beyond his independent state, its values, traditions, and culture. So he can only be a dignified human being if he lives in his country, where he defines the rule of order, elects the ruler, and manages his future.

A Georgian stood by his right to his state throughout history, from the Roman Empire till the Soviet Empire. We have seen twenty-five centuries of martyrdom, heroism, and sacrifice as Georgian men and women chose to die for their country; the road they took was astonishing and miraculous. And here we are, standing at the end of this road, ready to take a new pathway and start a fresh era."

Zurab Zhvania, *Privilege of My Generation*, Tbilisi, 1997

EUROPE OR ASIA?

"I am Georgian therefore I am European"—in this one sentence Zurab Zhvania, Georgia's late prime minister, summed up the country's national identity and foreign policy. Today Georgia is seeking closer ties with and eventual membership of NATO. Membership in the EU as a long-term priority.

As Zhvania said, history defines individuals and nations, so Georgia's desire to integrate into Europe has been shaped by the country's turbulent past. The Georgian psyche reflects the continual conquests and struggles for independence. Enemies and conquerors came from all sides: Persians, Arabs, Turks, Mongols. However, the most ferocious invaders were Tamerlane in the late fourteenth century and the Safavid Shah Abbas in the early seventeenth century. Because of these traumatic experiences, Georgians associate the Far and Middle East as well as Asia with the wars of the past, with their enemies, and the fear of losing their identity and religion.

Two centuries ago, as the Russian Empire expanded, it reached Georgia. But Georgians saw this as less of a threat since coming from *ertmortsmune*— Georgian for "the people of the same beliefs." They saw the first treaty with Russia as a replacement for their long-lost Christian ally the Byzantine Empire. But what followed shocked and outraged Georgians: in 1811, the independent (autocephalous) status of the Georgian Church was abolished by the Russian authorities. The small country had naively thought that it would enjoy some protection from Russia. The nineteenth century opened with the proclamation of the Russian Tsar incorporating Georgia into the Empire. In the twentieth century Georgia saw Bolshevik invasions and occupation of its territories.

After Soviet rule ended, tensions between the two countries climaxed—the Georgians blamed Russia for their loss of control over South Ossetia and Abkhazia. In 2008, the five-day Russia–Georgia war was the final nail in the coffin.

So don't be surprised if the Georgians do not take it as a compliment when foreigners say that their country is part of Asia, rather than Europe. Or when they do not like hearing that they should be close friends with Russia, rather than search for allies among the NATO countries. Of course, on an individual basis Georgians and Russians often get on well, especially as those who went to Soviet schools share a common language. But beyond this façade of cultural ties lies a big gap created by historical mistrust and resentment. If you look at their personal qualities, family values, and attitudes, a Georgian resembles an Arab, a Persian, or a Turk more than a European. But Georgians would rather describe themselves as being like the Spanish, Greeks, or Italians than admit sharing values and traditions with their former invaders. People in Georgia argue that the Black Sea culture is closer to the Mediterranean than to its immediate neighbors.

Dr. Adrian Brisku, author of *Albanian and Georgian Discourses on Europe*, describes the Georgian character as "colourful, generous, expressive and artistic," suggesting that Christianity brings Georgians and Europeans together, while geography sets them apart.

He continues, "There is no unanimity among Georgians about their Europeanness. If one considers the debates of Georgian intellectuals and politicians—from the making of the modern Georgian nation to the present—this question is answered in three ways: yes, we are Europeans because of a shared history, identity and destiny; no, we are Asians because unlike Europeans we have spirituality and intimate links with Eastern civilisations; and something in-between—Georgian culture has been marked and enriched by the influences of both East and West."

Georgians often compare their country to Janus, the Roman god of beginnings and transitions, who looks in different directions with two faces. They like saying that sandwiched between Europe and Asia, Georgia has the best of both—East and West. They also enjoy pointing out that the Silk Road has enriched their dishes with Mediterranean and Southeast Asian flavors. But for them the Asian influence is more of a color, an additional touch. They know much less about Asian or Middle Eastern literature than European; they encourage their children to travel to the West and learn Western languages rather than to look to the East.

REGIONAL DIFFERENCES

The Georgian psyche is the product not only of external conquests but also internal struggles. Regional and subcultural affiliations are sometimes stronger than national identity, and in the past feudal lords in west and east Georgia fought continuous wars with each other. There is also a big gap between the urban and rural populations—even though it is a small country, the lifestyle, attitude to traditions, and manner of speech in Tbilisi are significantly different from those in rural Guria, five to six hours' drive away from the capital. According to 2011 data, 57 percent of the population in the capital had gone on to higher education, as opposed to 16 percent in the countryside.

What unites all Georgians, however, is devotion and loyalty is to their families, first of all to the immediate nucleus and then to the wider circle of relations. Georgian identity is tied up with solidarity and patriotism—a Georgian always sees himself as part of a family, a group, a neighborhood, a class, a team, or a nation; he is ready to speak up and fight for them and expects to be supported when in need.

LANGUAGE, HOMELAND, RELIGION

Ilia Chavchavadze (1837–1907), one of the greatest Georgian writers, a public benefactor, and leader of the national liberation movement, posited three pillars—language, homeland, and religion—as the foundation of Georgian national identity. Known as the Pater Patriae (Father of the Fatherland) of modern Georgia, he called these the three treasures that make up a Georgian.

The Georgian language is closely tied in with national identity. A member of the South Caucasian language family, it is a tongue that a Georgian shares only with his compatriots. So Georgians feel very strongly that they alone "own" their language.

For a Georgian, there is no better place than his country. "Homeland" means the whole kingdom as well as his own piece of land that gives him food and wine. He feels very passionate about this small country sandwiched between huge empires. He utterly believes that invaders come to this land not just to extend their influence, but because Georgia is so special, so beautiful.

For a Georgian, Christianity is not just a religion: it is a symbol of defiance, as his fathers and forefathers have fought for their faith.

Language

While, in the nineteenth century, the Russian elites spoke French to their children, the Georgian nobility made sure their offspring were educated in Russian at the best schools in the Empire. It would, however, have been unthinkable for a Georgian man to speak Russian, French, or any other language than Georgian, to his children.

Currently, Georgians use Russian and English words in everyday speech. Some groups campaign to clean up the language, while others say that it is natural to adopt foreign words. Most Georgians will tell you one thing, though: Georgian has been spoken in this land since ancient times, and while many other languages have long since died out, theirs has survived. So there is no greater shame for a Georgian than not teaching his language to his children, whether they are living in Russia, Europe, or the USA.

Religion

The overwhelming majority of Georgians are Orthodox Christian. According to a recent national opinion poll, 98 percent of Georgian citizens declare that they believe in God. Out of those, 91 percent think that the institution of religion is important, while the remaining 9 percent simply believe in God's existence but do not connect their faith to religious rituals.

The Orthodox Church
Georgian Orthodoxy has been the state religion of Georgia since the fourth century, and it remains the dominant faith in the land. As a result of the Soviet Union's drive to eliminate religion, ancient churches were destroyed all over the country. After the collapse of the USSR in 1991, however, Georgia embraced religion, and the Georgian Orthodox Church has gone from strength to strength.

In 1917, there were 2,455 churches in Georgia, as well as monasteries, nunneries, church schools, and other institutions such as libraries, relic collections, and church archives. After the Red Army entered the country in 1921, the Communist regime gradually eliminated most churches, turning some of them into libraries, schools, shops, offices, or even public baths.

In 1945, up to fifty churches remained intact—mainly the old ones, retained as part of the national

cultural heritage, though most were museums rather than places of worship.

In 1974, following the liberal wave of the 1960s, some churches and monasteries were restored and services were regularly conducted in forty of them. In 1982, the number of functioning churches had risen to eighty. Today there are 1,100 cathedrals in Georgia, 130 nunneries, 165 monasteries, and up to sixty Georgian Orthodox churches outside the country.

The head of the Georgian Orthodox Church, Patriarch Ilia II, is a highly respected figure. When he promised personally to baptize any baby born to parents of more than two children, the country's birth rate increased by nearly 20 percent.

HOSPITALITY AND GENEROSITY

Dr. Levan Ghambashidze of Ilia State University, Tbilisi, who has studied modern Georgian national identity, maintains that Georgian values revolve around hospitality. "Georgians are proud of the cuisine; we believe that our country is the cradle of wine. Put this together and you will see that our values derive from the desire to treat our guests, be it the family or friends. Georgians are very particular about preserving their cultural heritage. Folk songs and dances are the source of individual pride for every Georgian. It's not that we think that other people cannot sing, dance, cook and treat their guests well. It's just that Georgians think that this is what we do better than anything else."

Another contemporary historian notes that he has been unable to find any reference to roadside hotels, taverns, or restaurants in Georgian manuscripts.

"Whenever there was a need to stop for a rest, travellers would just knock on the door of the first ordinary house they came across. They knew that they would be offered whatever the host had to give them, so there was no need to develop an infrastructure for travellers."

"Guests are sent by God," Georgians say. Hospitality is a religion in the country; it is enshrined in traditions; hosts go out of their way to please guests.

Too Much For Some

Georgian blogger Dato Parulava recently ridiculed the older generation for their out-of-date habits, writing:

"Many people still believe that one should be ready for guests to pop in at any moment; a good housewife should have something hidden in the cupboard for unannounced visits. So there is no need for the guests to call and inform the host in advance. Even if the host has no time or is not in the mood to welcome the visitors, seeing them enter his place will make him feel better. The family will send the child to the nearest supermarket to get some food (if they have no cash the child has to stop by the neighbor's and borrow some money on his way). Paradoxical, but true: in our country the host and the guest complain about inflation and rising food prices as they sit at the table overloaded with food."

The contemporary Georgian painter Eteri Chkadua links the cult of the woman to the cult of the guest in Georgia. Men open doors for women, do not let them carry their luggage, help to put on their coats, and pick up the checks in restaurants. That's the cult of the woman for you. But then there's also the cult of the guest: Georgian men will open their doors to guests at any time, as hospitality and generosity are the lifeblood of a Georgian. And when there is a visitor it is the woman who has to cook dinner and serve the company.

WOMEN IN SOCIETY

"The Women are so beautiful, that they seem born to inspire love; Yet they all paint their faces, and particularly their eyebrows, as if nature had been most unpropitious to their charms. They dress in a very ornamental style, in a Persian habit, and their hair is set off to advantage. They are witty, affable and complimentary, but naturally prone to deceit and cruelty," wrote Sir John Chardin, in *The Travels of Sir John Chardin through Mingrelia and Georgia into Persia*. As he reached Tehran in 1673 he concluded: "There is scarce a Gentleman in Persia, whose Mother is not a Georgian, or a Circassian Woman; to begin with the King, who commonly is a Georgian by the Mother's side."

Traditionally Georgian society is firmly patriarchal, and women have more honor than rights. The worst abuse you can throw at a Georgian man is to swear in a way that insults his mother. Georgian society understands and excuses a man who physically attacks someone if a female member of his family has been verbally abused. Men are expected to protect and provide for their women.

According to a survey conducted by the Caucasus Research Resource Center (CCRC) in 2010 "only

1 percent of Georgians say that the main decision maker at home should be a woman, and only 2 percent consider a female an ideal breadwinner." A majority of the Georgian population do not expect "a woman to drink strong alcohol, smoke tobacco, have premarital sex or live separately from her parents." So clearly Georgia is a traditional society with different behavioral norms expected from men and women. The situation is not as simple as it seems, though, as more women than men are primary breadwinners in Georgian families. Tbilisi cafés are full of young girls and their boyfriends, smoking and drinking after a day's work at high-profile organizations.

She Visits Him

Georgian women have a reputation for being more down-to-earth and practical than the men. Men always joke that Georgian girls are very result-oriented—for them marriage is the ultimate goal. Hence this anecdote about a Georgian girl's first visit to her beau's place:

As she enters his apartment, he looks at her and thinks, "Oh, she looks fabulous. I hope we make love and she stays over tonight." She smiles at him, scans the corridor very quickly, and thinks, "These shelves are too old, they will have to go; we need a walk-in wardrobe here; it won't be difficult to organize as soon as I move in. "

"A strong majority of Georgians say that women should not face obstacles receiving an education or finding work… And some 60 percent of Georgians are comfortable with the idea of having a female boss."

(Mariam Naskidashvili, *How Does Gender Determine Roles and Behaviors of Women In and Outside Georgian Families?*). The CRRC concludes that Georgia is not as straightforwardly conservative as it first seems. Young people, especially those who live in the capital, are educated, they have lived or traveled abroad, and tend to make a mockery of gender stereotypes. "It is possible that these seeming deeply entrenched attitudes may be changing."

ATTITUDES TOWARD AUTHORITY

Historically, the Georgians loved their monarchs. Today Georgian Orthodox Christians still pray for the rulers of the state, their subordinates, its army and its police, whoever they are. According to the historian Gio Akhvlediani, feudal lords and kings were father figures for Georgian peasants. Serfs called them "masters," a word loaded with positive connotations.

Nowadays, Georgians tend to identify political institutions with the main actors rather than the systems; parliament and political parties are often associated with individual political leaders and not with the ideologies underpinning them.

The Georgians like strong leaders, but they also love rebels. Georgian literature is full of exciting tales of kings and heroes who stood above the others and were distinguished by their dedication to their motherland. At the same time, in both folk and formal literature you will see great respect for the characters who led rebellions and uprisings or refused to obey orders from their tribe or superiors.

Levan Ghambashidze points out that attitudes toward authority changed as the authorities changed in the last century, and that Georgians are still very wary when it comes to the authorities.

EDUCATION

There is a long tradition of learning in Georgia. Historically, giving their children the best possible education was a central value for Georgians. In the old days it was believed that the best dowry for a Georgian noblewoman was her manuscripts, hand-copied by herself, of verses from the Bible and from the *Vefxistkaosani*, the Georgian epic tale of the twelfth century. This showed that her family

possessed the two most important books, that she could read and write, that before getting married she had spent time creating her own copies, and that she was bringing them to her new household. It also indicated that she would be able to

educate her children and pass the knowledge on to future generations. While some women made manuscripts of one chapter only, others had whole books ready to take with them. And if the bride's family were really rich, her copies would be bound within a silver or gold hard cover, decorated with precious stones. Most Georgian parents think that educating their children is their core mission. (More on this in Chapter 5.)

STATUS

Respect for the elderly is an important virtue for Georgians. The young are expected to rise when an older person enters the room. It is important to greet older people with reverence and to use Mr. and Mrs. when talking to people of one's parents' age or above. Anyone with a higher position or status also has to be addressed using the polite pronoun or verb forms in Georgian.

For older people status derives from being a member of the intelligentsia, whose ranks include only university professors. Most young people, however, believe that art and showbiz celebrities are the cream of society and enjoy an even higher status. There are those who argue that people with posts in government are worthy of greater respect because they are the decision makers, influencing the future of the country. Increasingly wealth and links to the upper echelons become a significant factor in defining a place in the social "who's who." But, even though Georgians like big cars and designer sunglasses, it is success and not mere wealth that commands respect and acknowledgment.

Until recently, the *kanonieri qurdi*, the so-called "thief in law" (criminal who obeys the thieves' code), escaped justice after committing an honor crime. Apart from having godfather status in the world of crime, these figures were highly esteemed by the public. During Soviet times the state was associated with injustice and outlaws were often admired for their independence and resilience. This perception has changed dramatically in the past five years, as most former gangsters turned businessmen have been arrested and zero tolerance has been declared toward honor crimes. Georgians admire strong individuals and being outstanding in any sense means popularity in some parts of society.

NAMUSI

Namus, Arabic for "virtue," means "dignity" in Georgian. The concept predates Islam, Christianity, or Judaism. In Arabic as well as some other languages the word can mean law, honor, or respect for customs. In Georgian it's a combination of these. At the same time it is absolute that the *namusi* of a man is determined by the integrity of all the women in his family. The man is considered less respectable if his sister, daughter, or mother, let alone his wife, has sex outside marriage, as faithfulness is one of the synonyms of *namusi*.

WORK ETHIC

The Georgian attitude toward office work can be very laid-back by Western standards. Mark Mullen, an American who has lived in Tbilisi for more than a decade, says that Georgians often think mornings are something to be endured, while evenings are a period to enjoy.

"Georgians stay up late, watching TV or just spending time with their friends or family, rarely waking up before nine a.m. If their phone rings in the morning, they get scared, thinking there is an emergency, something that could not wait till later. Tbilisi gears up late in the morning: at seven or eight the streets are deserted, by nine you will see some parents, but not too many of them, walking their children to school. Officially life starts at ten—until then most shops and offices are closed. However, for many, even ten is just an optional start time; it is a guideline rather than a rule. In reality Georgians show up at work around eleven . . . or . . . well, twelvish. This arrangement can be uncomfortable for foreigners used to doing regular office hours. Deal with it." (Mark Mullen, in the Georgian magazine *Liberali*, September 2011.)

Another American says that during his decade in Tbilisi he has met many experienced foreign bosses who came to the country with high ambitions to reorganize and transform this friendly but lax work culture. "They all realized that it was either not worth it or not possible. Yes, Georgians come to work quite late and they break for lunch shortly after they start their day, their lunch hour lasts for longer than sixty minutes, but at the end of the day they can deliver. Their country operates in a different you-do-something-for-me-and-I'll-help-you-later and my-brother-is-friends-with-your-cousin way." (Mike Twin, business consultant)

Seeing the bright side of Georgian work culture was more difficult for a London-based PR consultant. He constantly complained that his clients—major companies in Russia, Kazakhstan, Ukraine, and Georgia—refused to think ahead. "I do not mean to insult anyone, but because of their shared Soviet past, they never develop future strategies and only deal with the problems as they emerge. All the CEOs from the post-Soviet countries refuse to listen when I talk to them about building the company's image. They call me in a panic when they need my help with crisis management but then ignore me in 'peaceful times.' This probably arises from the uncertainty of the Soviet era, when there was no point in investing any time or energy in the future."

PUNCTUALITY AND APPOINTMENTS

Non-Georgian staff at the Tbilisi office of a major multinational corporation said that their local colleagues operated in a special time zone: GMT, or Georgian Maybe Time. Everything they planned was "around morning," or "sometime in the evening"— and even those vague plans were altered at short notice. In summer, as it gets very hot, most middle-class people with full-time jobs and stable incomes move out of the capital and commute to work from their vacation homes. One foreign consultant found that his summer business trip to Georgia was not half as productive as he had hoped. This is what he said: "I discovered that in summer they have longer commutes to work, so they come to the office later and leave earlier to go to their 'dachas'. . . the city grinds to a halt when it is very hot . . . I even got an out of office reply to my important e-mail, saying: 'Sorry, might take some time to reply, it's August.'"

DIVERSITY AND THE LIMITS OF TOLERANCE

In a conservative society that revolves around tradition and the family unit, homosexuals find it very hard to live openly. Traditions are strictest in mountainous region on the border with the Russian republic of Chechnya. In September 2011 the Russian Interfax News agency reported that "German tourists, who turned out to be gay, were beaten and thrown into a river in the mountain village of Omalo." The tourists had been invited to join a party at a local restaurant. Later, when they started kissing passionately after a traditional Georgian toast to love, the couple were physically set upon by their drunken hosts. According to the agency, no criminal investigation was launched into the incident as "The tourists quickly left Georgia, without complaining either to the Georgian police, or to the German Embassy in Tbilisi."

Tbilisi is home to up to one hundred different ethnic groups, including significant numbers of Armenians and Azeris and small groups of Ossetians, Abkhazians, Ukrainians, Greeks, Jews, Russians, Estonians, Germans, Kurds, Assyrians, and others. However, ethnic Georgians still dominate the political landscape as well as public life. Unlike Russia, Georgia has no tradition of anti-Semitism. But even though minorities are not discriminated against, it is obvious that Georgian people take more pride in their nationality than in mere citizenship.

Religious and public venues for peoples of various faiths and ethnicities are mainly concentrated in the old city. Your tour guide will tell you that in the Georgian capital, during the celebration of mass in the Armenian Church, or over the chants of the synagogue service, the call of the muezzin can be heard from the nearby mosque. Georgians are proud that different places of worship are within walking distance of each other. Nevertheless, the reality is that mixed marriages are quite rare and that Georgians know very little about Catholicism, Judaism, or Islam.

In the past, Russian was the only shared language between Georgians and the Armenian or Azeri communities. Nowadays, as young Georgians learn English rather than Russian, communication with non-Georgian-speakers has become a problem. Even though there are a lot of programs supporting the teaching of Georgian in minority schools, the gap between the ethnic groups is widening.

chapter three

TRADITIONS, FESTIVALS, & CUSTOMS

In Georgia, the year is defined by a round of festivals, celebrations, birthdays, and weddings. People prepare with great joy for major events. Georgians celebrate togetherness with huge enthusiasm; for them personal identity is tied up with the family, the group, the nation, solidarity, and patriotism. It is strongly believed that the support of loved ones makes it easier to endure hardships; it is also taken for granted that good times can only be good enough if they are enjoyed in wider company. So the social calendar for a Georgian is busy: the wedding of a cousin's neighbor one week, the baptism of a colleague's newborn the week after, and the funeral of a grandparent's friend some time in between. Even though it is a secular country, religious festivals are eagerly looked forward to by most people. And once they get around the table Georgians give in to food and wine, interrupted only by toasts, songs, dances, anecdotes, and laughter.

NEW YEAR

The New Year is celebrated with fireworks and champagne at the stroke of midnight across the whole country. Most Georgians usually stay at

home till midnight and leave to see friends right after the clock strikes twelve. Some young people go to the main square and greet the coming year in front of the central Christmas tree. Afterward, Georgians spend all night partying, going from one house to another and drinking at each party. The guests are supposed to bring candies and chocolates, while the hosts are expected to treat them with homemade delicacies:

- *Gozinaki*—traditional New Year sweets, made at home exclusively on December 31. Caramelized hazelnuts and walnuts, fried in honey, fill the air and add a special touch to the celebration.
- *Churchkhela*—jokingly called Georgian Snickers, made by sewing walnuts on to a string, dipping them in thickened grape juice, and drying. Because of its nutritious value, it was very popular among Georgian soldiers, who would take *churchkhela* to battle. Even though it is made during the grape harvest, it is not eaten until December 31.
- *Satsivi*—a traditional New Year's Day dish, served on January 1, it is similar to Thanksgiving turkey, but served in walnut sauce.

While on New Year's Eve most restaurants are open all night and offer a colorful live show along with food and wine, almost all are closed on the first day of the year. New Year's Eve is mainly spent among friends, but January 1 is a family day. After waking up late in the afternoon, families sit down for a traditional, generously laid feast with *satsivi* at the center of the meal. As a rule the eldest sibling or parents host the dinner for the extended family. In most cases the main feature in the dining room is not just a Christmas tree but also the TV, which for Georgians is almost like a family member. Throughout the year they like keeping the TV set turned on all the time, even when no one is watching. But it is an absolute must on January 1 as the special end-of-year programs are an inseparable part of the festival.

On this day children expect a surprise visit from Tovlis Babu, a local equivalent of Santa Claus. The Georgian Santa wears a shepherd's coat and carries a brightly decorated double sack bulging with gifts.

OLD STYLE HOLIDAYS

January 2 is a very auspicious day. Georgians believe that whatever they do on this day will shape the coming year, as this is the Day of Fate. Even those who are not superstitious try to have as much fun as possible, as this is considered a good omen.

After New Year's Eve, New Year's Day, and the Day of Fate, the country gears up to celebrate Christmas (January 7) and then old style New Year. The Orthodox Church still operates using the Julian calendar, even though it was replaced by the Gregorian calendar at the beginning of the twentieth century. So January 13 sees a less flamboyant repetition of the New Year festival. And January 14 is another chance for extended families to toast the coming year and wish each other health, wealth, and success.

NATIONAL HOLIDAYS	
1–2 January	New Year's Day
7 January	Orthodox Christmas
19 January	Orthodox Epiphany
3 March	Mother's Day
8 March	International Women's Day
Movable	Good Friday, Easter, and Easter Monday
9 April	Restoration of Independence Day, Commemoration Day of the Fallen
9 May	Victory Day
12 May	St. Andrew's Day
26 May	Independence Day
28 August	St. Mary's Day (Assumption of the Virgin)
14 October	Mtskhetoba, commemorating fifth-century capital of Georgia
23 November	St. George's Day

CHRISTMAS

Although there are not that many non-Orthodox Christians in Georgia, December 25 is celebrated quite widely as "Western Christmas," not only by Catholic and Protestant communities, but by liberal Georgians. Some Orthodox believers condemn the marking of this day, as they think it is disrespectful to what they call real Christmas, two weeks later. Even if people do not celebrate on this

day, it still marks the beginning of the long seasonal holidays that last for almost a month. Foreigners are often shocked when they discover that Georgians celebrate Christmas and New Year twice in such a short period. There is little point in planning a business trip to Georgia in early January, as it is only toward the end of the first month of the year that the country awakens after a long festive season and slowly returns to normal routine.

On Orthodox Christmas Eve, January 6, you will see processions of the faithful in the streets, called *Alilo*, singing traditional carols and collecting for charity. Devout believers go to church for a celebratory mass. On Christmas Day there is plenty of food and wine but fewer gifts than on New Year's Day. Most families have already opened presents by this time and, though they spend the day together, they still tend to think of Christmas as a religious celebration, which has to be joyful but subdued.

EASTER
Easter in Georgia is associated with red eggs and Easter cakes. Hard-boiled eggs are colored on

Good Friday, three days before Easter Sunday. Most believers fast for forty days before Easter, attend church on Saturday evening for the special mass (the Liturgy for Dismissals), and spend all night there. In the morning they gather together and break their fast. The concept of the Orthodox fast is to refrain from eating animal products, to avoid arguing, and to abstain from sex. You will find that many people take up a vegan diet before important Christian festivals (Christmas, Easter, St. Mary's Day) and they organize extravagant feasts to celebrate the end of the fasting period and the festival itself.

At Easter people greet each other with the words "Christ has risen," and answer by saying, "Risen indeed." Then they take their Easter eggs (real, not chocolate!) and hit them against each other. The ones that break must be shared around. Children get the smallest and strongest eggs, as the aim is not to break the shell of your egg.

Easter Monday

On Easter Monday, most Georgians go to the cemetery to pay their respects to deceased relatives and friends. People take flowers, wine, and some food to the graves of loved ones and to meet friends there. Sometimes they drink a glass or two to toast the dead and the living. Graves in Georgia often have benches and small tables around them and it is common for relatives to spend time, eat, and drink at the cemetery. The way in which Georgians decorate the gravestones and carry out post-life rituals shows the strong influence of pre-Christian traditions.

OTHER HOLIDAYS
Mother's Day vs Women's Day
After Georgia gained its independence from the
Soviet Union, March 8, International Women's Day,
was abolished along with other Soviet festivals.
Instead, March 3 was introduced to celebrate
motherhood, maternal bonds, and the influence
of mothers in society. Many criticized this move,
saying that it discriminated against single and
childless women. As a result, the holiday was
reinstated and now Georgians celebrate both days.
On March 3 as well as March 8, all women receive
flowers: people celebrate not just feminine beauty,
but also the beginning of spring.

April 9 and May 26
Georgia celebrates Independence Day on May 26 to
mark the establishment of the Democratic Georgian
Republic (1918–21). The GDR was short-lived and
was followed by seventy years under the USSR.
Independence was restored on April 9, 1991, and the
country marks Restoration of Independence Day on
April 9. This day is also called the Day of National
Unity as independence came after the Tbilisi
Massacre of April 9, 1989. For many the April
tragedy is synonymous with the fight for freedom
and is the Georgian equivalent of Tiananmen Square.

WEDDINGS
Traditional Georgian weddings start in the
afternoon, when the groom's family and friends visit
the bride's house and take her to the church. After
the religious ceremony they all go to the civil
register office to tie the knot there. Later, the party

moves to a restaurant for dinner and entertainment. Depending on how close you are to the family, you might be invited to participate from the very beginning or join in at some point during the day. If you plan to give money or gold, you do not have to discuss it with the couple in advance. If, however, you choose to present the second most popular type of gift— a kitchen appliance or something for their home—make sure to mention it in advance as someone else might have offered the same thing.

According to an old tradition, in the past the groom and his friends would ride on horseback to the girl's home; there they would have drinks with the girl's family, and she would be brought out only later, when it was time to leave. Then they would all rush to the church, with the couple's carriage at the front of the convoy. It was believed that whoever arrived first after the carriage was the bravest and most devoted friend of the couple, so young men would compete with each other to demonstrate their dedication. On their way to the church one of the groom's friends would ask the rest of the company, "Who is this beautiful girl?" And they would reply with the popular wedding folk song "This beauty is ours."

Do not be surprised if, similarly, on the way from the church to the civil register office or to the restaurant, your Georgian friends start making crazy maneuvers to ensure their car does not fall behind. There is no Georgian wedding without a wedding race; the competition gets so fierce that some people do not mind scratching their cars as long as they are first among the guests.

Georgian wedding parties are lavish and entertaining but, with two to three hundred people attending them, they are extremely rowdy. In the past, as she would enter her new home, the bride would step on a plate and break it on the threshold for good luck. Now it is done as she enters the

restaurant. Single bridesmaids often grab a piece of the plate as they believe they will see their future husband in a dream if they put it under their pillow that night. The party begins with the best man inviting the bride for a traditional dance; after a few moves, the groom steps in and the best man leaves the stage. After the first dance the guests can join in.

Historically, the practice of bride kidnapping was commonplace in rural Georgia. The groom, together with his friends, would abduct a woman he wished to marry. Later, this tradition was used to justify elopement—the couple would run away together but the girl's parents would be told that she had been married by "capture." After a month of hiding from the girl's relatives, the couple would return from the honeymoon in the hope that there would be no reprisals by her relatives as by that time she was expecting his baby. Today, bride capture is illegal, but sometimes "abduction" happens with the consent of the bride and her parents, to avoid the expense of a traditional wedding. Even though the tradition is now well in the past, at Georgian weddings you can still hear the popular folk song "We are coming overjoyed with pride as we have snatched the most beautiful bride."

BIRTHDAYS AND NAME DAYS

Birthdays in Georgia are marked in the same way as in the West. If invited to a celebration, you will not be expected to pay for your drinks or club entry. Normally the birthday boy or girl (or their parent or partner) organizes everything and the guests are free to enjoy themselves. As Georgians consider it inappropriate to open gifts in front of others, do not be surprised if the host quickly puts your box in a pile without even looking at it; the recipient will get back to you a day later to thank you.

Georgians also celebrate their name days (also known as angels' days). People who are named for a saint normally mark the saint's day and receive cards or presents. Name celebrations can be very confusing as some of the saints have more than one day in the Orthodox calendar, so you will hear again and again that Anna, Nino, Mariam, or Tamara are celebrating their name days. If your Georgian girlfriend is named after a saint, say Anna or Nino, she probably expects flowers on Anaoba (Anna's Day) or Ninaoba (Nino's Day).

Men do not mark name days as often as women. David and George, however, are the most popular Georgian names as well as the most important saints, so Davitoba (David's Day) or Giorgoba (George's Day) is a big celebration for everyone, not only those who are named after them. Georgian names have numerous variations: Gogi, Giga, Gigi, Gicho, and Gogita are short forms for George, while Maro, Meri, Masho, Masha, Mari, Mariana, Marina, Maria, Marisha, and Marika might all stand for Mariam (Georgian for Mary). In order not to get confused by diminutives, you can ask what a person's full Christian name is and pleasantly surprise them by congratulating them on their saint's day.

FUNERALS

Depending where they take place, funerals can vary considerably. There are, however, some general rules that apply to rural as well as urban families. Immediately after a person dies, close family and friends come together at home or in the church. They choose two days for receiving condolences and assign a day for the burial. Then they spend the intervening time mourning and preparing for the "final day." This period usually lasts three to five days and is followed by the burial on a Tuesday, a Thursday, or on a weekend.

Religious ceremonies and prayers are conducted only in the presence of the close family. Two evenings before the burial, the doors of the bereaved family's house are open to everyone. People close to the deceased or to one of the family members pay short visits to offer their condolences. The family is seated in front of the coffin while visitors enter the room, walk slowly around the coffin, shaking hands with the men and nodding to the women. If possible, they talk to the person to whom they have come to express their sympathy and then leave.

The actual burial is attended by more people than is customary in the West. After the funeral it is common to sit down for a solemn but not extended meal in a modest restaurant. Everyone who has attended is invited to join in, so on such occasions one might see two to three hundred people, all dressed in black, dining in silence.

FUNERAL IN SAMEGRELO

In a small village on the border of Abkhazia and Samegrelo (Mengrelia), a teacher of English, who also worked as an interpreter with the international observers based in the region, lost her husband. Her foreign colleagues decided to pay her a visit to offer their condolences. As they entered the parlor where the body was laid out, the widow started crying out, in English.

"Bondo," she said to the dead man, "my colleagues are here. Mr. Barthwal, the head of our team, is just coming in, and he is followed by Mr. Gani, his deputy, as well as Mr. Gil, who joined our team only a month ago. Bondo, they are here for you. Please, rise and greet them, they are your guests!" she implored, with tears in her eyes.

This address shocked the visitors, who stood there not knowing what to do while she introduced them to her husband in his coffin. This story of three foreigners turning pale as the dead man was told to rise and greet them became a much repeated anecdote. The woman, however, simply wanted to thank each of her colleagues in person and also to express her deep sorrow on her husband's death.

RTVELI FESTIVALS

Rtveli is a festival of the grape harvest and wine making. It normally takes place in late September in grape-growing areas and usually lasts for several days: people who start picking and sorting grapes early in the morning, after hours of work end the day with a feast and folk songs.

REVELLING IN GEORGIA'S GRAPE

Former BBC correspondent Rob Parsons, who part owns a vineyard in Georgia, gives this account of the Rtveli:

"The vine in Georgia has an iconic significance unmatched anywhere else in the world. The vine is entwined into the national psyche—a symbol of regeneration, of wealth and plenty, and of the country's Christian faith in a sea of Islam and of resistance.

The Alazani valley lies on the old invasion route of the Persians into Georgia. The soldiers of the Shah would march along the road where our vineyard stands today hacking and burning as they advanced.

Yet just as often as the Persians destroyed the vines, the Georgians would grow them back again. Perhaps because of this, the grape harvest in Georgia is more than just a Dionysian celebration—although it is that as well. It is existential. It is a reaffirmation of survival, a statement of identity and of attachment to the land.

The *rtveli* also marks the end of the agricultural cycle; it is the last of the harvests. When it is over, preparation for the winter must begin.

Our pickers arrived not by horse and cart but on the back of a swaying lorry. They disgorged into the vineyard, wicker baskets on their backs and the picking began.

We worked all morning, plucking the swollen sticky fruit from their straining stems. By midday the job was done: 300 kilos [660 pounds] of grapes. Not a big crop this year, but the fruit was good. Enough perhaps for 150 litres [40 gallons] of wine.

That night we celebrated the end of the old and the beginning of a new cycle of life. We roasted kebabs on a bed of vine cinders and quaffed great draughts of last year's wine to an endless stream of toasts.

I stepped outside onto the balcony and into the great amphitheatre of the Alazani valley. A power cut [outage] had plunged the whole of Kakheti into darkness. Inside, the revellers were in full flow. 'What enmity has destroyed,' they sang, 'love will rebuild,' their words drifting out across the valley."

FOLKORE AND SUPERSTITIONS

Superstition is part of everyday life; it shapes customs and in a way even influences religious celebrations. Georgians often confuse St. George with the pagan deity White George. On St. Mary's Day, in rural areas children jump over fire to scare the devil. In the mountains they still mark Lomisoba, a bloody festival of lamb sacrifice. This is an example of how the Georgian psyche was created by overlaying pre-Christian with Christian beliefs: a church was built on the site of the pagan idol Lomisa and dedicated to St. George; the main icon in this church was given the name St. George of Lomisa by people who believed in its miraculous powers. Once a year, *mtiuli*—Georgians from the mountains (*mta* is "mountain" in Georgian)— come together for the Orthodox feast of St. Mary and perform rituals that have little to do with Christianity.

Sacrificing animals to ask God for the well-being of loved ones is common not only in the mountains but also in rural areas. This practice, strictly forbidden in Christianity, is always conducted not far away from churches and monasteries, so that the group can light a candle right after the creature is slaughtered. Afterward the participants sit down for a picnic, enjoy the meal, and toast the Creator.

There are many dishes that are not served on happy occasions, just because they are associated with grief. Wheat porridge, made of pearl barley, raisins, and walnuts, is cooked only when commemorating the dead; some people place the dish in front of the deceased's photograph and offer it to others afterward.

Young children often wear agate amulets to protect them from the evil eye—if an envious neighbor should look at a child wishing them ill, it is believed that the stone will absorb the negative energy and break, leaving the owner unharmed.

Georgians are very interested in interpreting their dreams. Friends or colleagues often tell each other what they dreamed the night before, in order to detect the message and explain the symbols.

When traveling, people tend to sit down in silence for a minute before leaving home, as going away in a hurry might lead to a chaotic trip. In the morning, after closing the door behind them, they avoid going back, even if they realize they have forgotten something. Returning is a bad omen, meaning that the day will be hectic and confused.

Not all superstitions are shared by all Georgians, but there is a tendency to believe in various signs and warnings. The importance given to omens will vary depending on a family's background and education, but most people have at least one or two superstitious habits that they follow without any rational explanation. Almost 100 percent of Georgian families avoid buying clothes and toys for an unborn baby; they do not throw a party on the child's first birthday (child mortality was quite high in the past and parents, frightened that their daughter or son would not survive deadly infectious diseases, did not want to tempt fate); and as a rule, most couples avoid tying the knot in May, which is a bad omen as it is believed that those married in May will divorce within a year.

Omens—Georgian Predictions

If you drop a fork, there will be an unexpected visitor knocking at your door.

If you spill some salt, there will be a fight; you need to laugh out loud to prevent it.

Breaking a mirror brings bad luck for seven years; sitting at the corner of a table means one will be single for another seven years.

If your hand is itchy, some cash is coming in; kiss your hand or the money might not reach you.

chapter four

MAKING FRIENDS

Georgians "inherit" some of their friends, as parents try to make sure that their children are close to the sons and daughters of their friends. Most links are formed through family ties or at school and last a lifetime; falling out is not very common, as friends are like family—even when people go different ways childhood friends are still special.

Georgian friends are in each other's pockets: they drop in uninvited and they stay for a long

time, not just to have fun but also to help with household chores, cooking, or babysitting. As ties are close, expectations are high. If a friend is a foreigner, however, people tend not to be as demanding. They like to open up and get close to non-Georgian friends; a visitor can be fully accepted. But locals will not expect the same level of intimacy with you at the initial stage. This will give you a chance to decide if you want to keep your distance or to embrace the friendship completely.

If you are visiting Georgia, be ready to be pampered, taken to see the sights, offered entertainment, food, and drinks. Also, be ready to say "no" more than once as Georgians consider that refusing the first offer is just an act of politeness. Your host will insist on your trying all sorts of local delicacies, drinking more than you can stand, and going from one place to another to show you "one more ancient church."

ATTITUDES TOWARD FOREIGNERS
Making friends in Georgia is easy. Most locals are welcoming to foreigners as hospitality is a core value for all the people of the Caucasus. *Uckho* means "foreign" in Georgian, though the word also indicates "interesting," "special," or "rare." In Soviet times anything that was uncommon was treasured. The term *uckho* is much more than a century old; it probably dates from the times when Georgia was on the Silk Road, which brought many foreign and thus interesting products into the country. Georgians like making friends with foreigners; they are curious and want to know as much as possible about you and your life abroad.

From their early childhood, Georgians are taught that outside their homes they represent their families and are ambassadors of their country if they go abroad. So, while interacting with foreigners, people try to make a positive impression, so that their guests go away with positive memories of their homeland. You will also be identified with the county you come from: people might assume that all your countrymen are like you, or that you know all the facts and figures concerning your native land. Be ready for specific questions about the geography, culture, and politics of your country. Your host might recite Byron if you come from England, or read a Georgian translation of Heinrich Heine if you are from Germany.

Those Georgians who have never traveled abroad think that all foreigners, especially Westerners, are richer and have more carefree lives. So if you want to find a hotel or book a taxi, it is important to do some research about the local rates. If you have Georgian friends helping to arrange the trip, spell out how much you are ready to pay, as they might otherwise go for the most expensive options simply because they want to provide the best. Also, be careful: some people try to rip off foreigners; others may just offer them the most exclusive choices.

In general, the attitude to foreigners is positive and people are helpful if a stranger wants to travel or settle down in their country. Note that Georgians find it very unpleasant if they are asked to criticize their homeland or countrymen in front of non-Georgians. So, if you travel as a journalist or on a fact-finding mission, it is worth remembering that Georgians think it important to support each other and not to "wash their dirty laundry in public." The same is true in the corporate environment, where foreign experts are welcome, but still regarded as outsiders.

If you stay in a guesthouse and make friends with the family, they might say that you do not need to pay, as it is considered rude to ask friends for money. You should, however, insist on making the payment as this offer is more of a gesture.

Keep in mind that Georgians believe it necessary to make polite offers.

Georgians generally consider that they are better friends than foreigners. They think of themselves as warmer, more supportive, compassionate, and caring. Most believe that the bonds of friendship in Western countries are not very strong, otherwise people would not share their problems with psychiatrists. Once they get to know you personally, it is easy to make real friends. When this happens, get ready for a compliment: they will surely say you are so kind, it seems you have a Georgian heart.

The Caucasus Research Resource Center conducted a survey into household composition, and social and political attitudes and practices in Georgia, Armenia, and Azerbaijan. Answering the question, "Would you approve of a woman of your ethnicity marrying a foreigner?" 41 to 45 percent of Georgians said yes, if the groom was from Russia, Ukraine, or Greece. It was revealed that Orthodox Christians are most welcome to marry into Georgian families, and other people of different Christian faiths are considered second-best. Only 19 percent of Georgians said they would welcome Chinese, Turkish, Indian, or Iranian sons-in-law. People are more liberal when it comes to doing business with foreigners, but more than half of those interviewed still said that they would not want to have Chinese or Kurdish business partners.

INVITATIONS HOME
If you are invited to a Georgian home your hosts will make sure they offer the best they have. People go out of their way to impress foreign guests; they

might even empty a master bedroom for you or borrow money in order to put on a special feast.

Your first visit is likely to be a full sit-down meal, where you will be toasted, indulged, and overfed. The next few visits could be the same or similar. If, later, you are offered tea in the kitchen, this means you have become a true friend.

If you receive an invitation to visit a Georgian household, it will be a phone call on short notice. Do *not* arrive on time as you will discover that your host was expecting you to be at least an hour later. Make sure you take gifts—flowers for the hostess, something sweet for the kids, or a souvenir from your own country. There will be no milling around with cocktail glasses and canapés. You will be asked to sit, without any predinner conversation, at an extravagantly laid table. This is most likely to consist of starters and cold dishes; the hostess will bring in the main courses later. The host will insist on giving you plenty to drink—the only excuse for not drinking would be your religious belief or a health condition.

Georgian culture revolves around eating and drinking, and wine is an essential part of the culture, but Georgians don't sip their wine like Europeans. As one vistor observed, "They throw it back with gusto, one glass at a time." Georgian hosts think it important that you leave their place drunk, but they will not like it if you get tipsy too quickly.

Stand-up buffets and receptions involving socializing and networking might be acceptable at corporate events, but partying in true Georgian style is either a picnic with barbecues or a proper sit-down meal. Jugging plates and nibbling on canapés is just not Georgian.

THE *SUPRA* AND THE *TAMADA*

For Georgians drinking is not just consuming alcohol; it is a dramatic ritual. This can be like a group counseling session or can appear like a sales presentation . . . it is hard to tell which. One can only have the experience and either hate or absolutely love the ceremony of food and wine sharing. A *supra*—a Georgian party—starts by appointing a *tamada*, or toastmaster, who runs the event.

After toasting friends and family, the *tamada* goes round the *supra* and suggests individual toasts to the guests. This is the moment when people are slightly inebriated after a few glasses and the Georgian *supra* turns into a supportive group therapy session. One after the other, the guests focus their full attention on one of their number,

not just saying "Cheers," but telling them how special they are. The occasion gives the participants permission to tell stories, express love and gratitude, remember how they first met each other, what was the most poignant moment in their relationship, and so on. It looks a bit like a therapy session because the full attention of the party moves from one person to the next. This ritual is very old and people tend to follow the rules with great respect; however, it is possible to improvise. One thing that is not allowed at a Georgian *supra* is a notebook, as a *supra* is supposed to be a spontaneous expression of love.

Unfortunately, as people get drunk, *supras* can become rowdy and unpleasant, but if you are in a small and cheerful company run by an experienced and creative toastmaster, it is possible to spend all evening singing, toasting, sharing food and wine, exchanging positive emotions, praising each other, and giving big hugs. Most Georgian families have a piano or a guitar in the dining room. Some guests who play the guitar well even take it with them when visiting others.

The hosts will consider the *supra* to be a failure if the *tamada* gets drunk before the guests. Or if the guests consume all the food—the table has to be full even after the guests are full. Empty serving trays are a sign of tightfisted and stingy hosts.

HUMOR
Georgians like joking, telling anecdotes, and impersonating others. Most popular anecdotes are about subcultures within the country, politics, or about love–hate relationships with their neighbors.

Three Wishes

God meets representatives of Armenia, Azerbaijan, and Georgia, offering each of them the fulfillment of one wish. The Armenian asks God to remove all Azeris from the region. Next in turn is the Azerbaijani, who pleads with God to make all the Armenians leave the Caucasus. At the end the Georgian is asked to make his wish known: "Dear God," he says, "I do not want to disturb you with my wish; just do what these two have asked."

You might hear this anecdote in all three countries of the South Caucasus. Depending on who tells it, however, the nationality of the clever guy changes.

Another from the same series explains the reasons why Georgians should not become world football (soccer) champions: overcome with joy, the Georgians would die as they would not be able to digest this information; envy would kill the Armenians; and it would be stupid to leave the Caucasus just to the Azeris. Again, depending on who tells the story, all the characters can be shuffled around.

During the Russian–Georgian war in August 2008—when Russian tanks invaded Georgia proper—the Georgian president, Mikhail Saakashvili, was interviewed by major international news channels one after the other. As he was waiting for the BBC interview to begin, he absentmindedly stuffed the end of his red silk tie in his mouth and began to chew it in an apparent attack of nerves. The Russian media ridiculed the president and questioned his sanity as they showed this video clip with the caption "Saakashvili eats his tie." But Georgians respond to critical situations with lighthearted humor. Shortly after the Russian tanks pulled out of Georgia, this joke became very famous: Saakashvili in a tie shop, "I want these two ties, please." Shop assistant, "Mr. President, do you want to eat in or take out?"

Flexibility, humor, and wit are said to be the key characteristics of the West Georgians, especially Mengrelians. Another anecdote tells of a Mengrelian who checked into a hotel abroad and found a mouse in his room. He did not speak enough English to complain properly, but still decided to talk to the receptionist. Not knowing what the word "mouse" was in English, he smiled to her and said, " You know Tom and Jerry? Well, Jerry is upstairs."

Cold War Humor

The culture of political anecdotes comes from Soviet times. This one is from the 1980s:
Eduard Shevardnadze (USSR Minister of Foreign Affairs) meets James Baker (US Secretary of State) during the Cold War talks.
Baker: You know we have democracy in the States. People can get together in a demonstration and criticize the US president.
Shevardnadze: You know we have the same liberties in the USSR. People are free to demonstrate and criticize . . . the US president.

DATING, GEORGIAN STYLE

If an unmarried Georgian couple is dating, this may or may not mean they have sex—young

Georgians can be very traditional, or, in the cities, quite liberal. As, in rural areas, young people do not move out of their parents' houses, here people tend to be more conservative.

Families will start investigating if their son is seeing a local girl. It is important to find out whether her family has a good reputation; it might be a problem if she or her mother (yes, a mother or a sister) had had too many boyfriends; in a small country like Georgia it is not hard to find out such details of others' private lives. People are less inquisitive about foreigners, however. They might not always want a daughter or son-in-law from abroad, because of the language barrier, but no one will start inquiring about the background of a foreign bride.

Georgia is full of stories about the gallantry and extravagance of local men, their romantic and old-fashioned style of courtship. Even though there are more women than men in the country, you will still hear of competition (even fights) among men to win a certain woman's heart.

Dating a Georgian woman is an expensive activity as she would not expect to pay for anything when invited out by a gentleman. If invited to meet the girl's family, the fiancé is expected to present flowers to the future mother-in-law.

If you are a foreign woman regularly dating a Georgian man, be ready to be shown to an endless number of his friends, family, relatives, and colleagues. People find it important to introduce their future partners to the whole world and get their opinion on the important decision.

PERSONAL SPACE AND BODY LANGUAGE

Georgians often ask direct questions. People think of privacy and personal space as less important than friendship and support. Georgians often make fun of foreigners who, they think, are more distanced and diplomatic with their friends. Expect to be asked: "You have been dating for a long time; when do you plan to get married?" "Now that you are married, do you plan to have children?" "Will you be having a child right away or later?" "Do you want to have just one child or more?

If Georgians want to go out, they do not have to look up agencies to find a babysitter for their kids. Friends, and even friends' parents, are ready to help. They will instantly, however, tell your child off if she or he is misbehaving. They are there to be concerned when you have flu, to intervene and help when you need it, to give advice, to demand that you follow it, and to criticize you if you don't.

What shocks foreigners most is Georgian body language and the expressive manner of talking. In the streets you will see people kissing and hugging; showing love is customary, not only between women: men also give each other a big kiss when they meet. In other circumstances, you might see them speaking in a very loud voice and using their hands for emphasis. There is nothing to worry about; they are not shouting at each other; they might not even be arguing. It is a normal "Georgian exchange."

Smiling at strangers is thought by locals to be a sign of mental disorder. Foreigners often find that smiling and not receiving a smile back is one of the weirdest things in Georgia. So be prepared not to get a reciprocal or welcoming beam from a shop assistant or a waitress. People rarely smile in the street.

The only exception is for children, who are doted on by everyone and are often given sweets by strangers. It is considered normal for a stranger to talk and play with a cute child, ask her name, tell her that her dress is gorgeous and that she looks like a little princess.

NEIGHBORS

For Georgians, neighbors are like relatives. In rural areas people never lock their doors and it is common for neighbors to walk in and join the family for a meal without any invitation. In the cities it has become more common to make arrangements in advance; however, spontaneous visits are still considered less formal and more friendly as they spare the host or hostess the obligation to cook. "We borrow salt from each other"—by this Georgian phrase people indicate that they are very close to their neighbors; salt can be a metaphor for other things than money.

LIVING ON KINDNESS

In her book *Stories I Stole from Georgia*, Wendell Steavenson, who lived in Tbilisi for two years, describes the city of the 1990s, when the worst crisis hit the Georgians:

"Venera, the older woman, was an indefatigable borrower: my telephone was her telephone and whether it was kerosene or a bit of garlic or an extra blanket or some coffee or a couple of cigarettes or a few balls of naphthalene or three eggs, I surrendered them to her. In return she knocked on my door at all hours and exhorted me to come and drink vodka with her and eat home-made raspberry jam; I usually went. I was very fond of vodka and home-made raspberry jam. . . . This was the city, it lived on kindness. Nurses often bought medicine for their patients with their own money, neighbours brought bread for neighbours, people pooled resources. A man who was earning well, a customs official, a policeman . . . a bureaucrat, a driver for the Western NGO, supported an extended family of several families. Friends gave friends overcoats or clothes for their children. If you had some money, there was someone who needed to borrow it. Half [of] Tbilisi owed the other half money."

SOME DOS AND DON'TS

- If invited to a Georgian household, do not ask what to bring. Your host would most definitely tell you that it is an insult to visit a Georgian family with a bottle or a food offering. However, you are not expected to take this literally and turn up empty-handed. Bring something from your home country: a box of chocolates, say (especially if you come from Switzerland), would probably be better appreciated than a local souvenir or delicacy.
- Do not start taking your shoes off when you enter your host's home. It is customary to offer slippers to visitors in neighboring Russia and Azerbaijan, but Georgian hosts will not like it if you are unaware that their culture is different from their neighbors'.

- Do not compare Georgia to any of its neighbors; this could lead to some very sensitive conversations. If you are asked whether Georgia belongs more to Europe or Asia, do not say that the country is more Asian than European. This is not what what your hosts would be happy to hear.

- Do not try to use Russian in order to impress your hosts. It's better to say "Cheers" than "*Za zdarovie.*" But "*Gaumarjos*" would be best.

- Do not empty your glass or finish the food on your plate unless you want to be offered more.

- Most Georgians do not mind others smoking at the table, so some smoke while others eat or drink. However, blowing one's nose in public is considered extremely rude, especially if there are people eating in the room.

Talking About Stalin

> ### Morning
> *The Rose's bud had blossomed out, reaching out*
> *   to touch the violet*
> *The lily was waking up, bending its head*
> *   in the breeze*
> *High in the clouds the lark was singing a*
> *   chirruping hymn*
> *While the joyful nightingale with a gentle voice*
> *   was saying—*
> *"Be full of blossom, oh lovely land! Rejoice*
> *   Iverian's country*
> *And you, oh Georgian, by studying, bring joy to*
> *   your motherland."*
>
> Soselo (transl. by Donald Rayfield)

It is hard to find a Georgian who has not read, heard, or memorized this verse by Ioseb Jughashvili. Written under his pen name, Soselo, it symbolizes Stalin's prerevolutionary youth.

Few imagined than that this ordinary Georgian lad would come to dominate world politics. The story of the young Georgian from the small town of Gori who became the ruler of a vast and powerful empire still fills some of his compatriots

with pride. If you want to tell them how bloody this empire was, be ready to hear their counterarguments about the turbulent times and that "he had no choice" or "he himself did not know." So disputes about Stalin might lead to uncomfortable and unpleasant conversations. You will be surprised that some Georgian people are very remote from a Western European interpretation of history.

Stalin is by no means a taboo topic, however—on the contrary, people are ready to talk and share their opinions about him. Some people will argue to defend "the great leader"; others will condemn the purges and massacres but may still think highly of Stalin's personal virtues, strategic thinking, and survival skills. You will find that Georgians do not shy away from conversations about Stalin, and even Hitler; they find it interesting to offer their views and to hear what you have to say, without any political correctness, so prevalent in the West.

Friendly Greeting

"My grandfather first visited Berlin as a young Soviet soldier during the Second World War. Recently he came again to visit me and my German husband Joseph in our Berlin apartment. In his late seventies, Grandpa was still full of energy, always ready to go sightseeing with me and my spouse. The two of them did not share a language to have proper conversations, but most of the time I was there to translate and act as a mediator. One night, Grandpa woke up and decided to go to the lavatory. It was past midnight but Joseph was still watching TV. Grandpa did not expect to come across anyone in the dining room so he was probably startled to see him. I assume my grandfather decided he had to say something, and as his vocabulary was very limited, he gave Joseph a broad smile and hailed 'Heil Hitler.' Afterward, he realized that his joke had not gone over very well, but he was unable to pin down why his beloved son-in-law was so shocked. The next day I had a hard time explaining Joseph's reaction to the old man. 'It was just a joke, what's wrong with that?' he repeated with a smile."

S. K. C.

REVERSE CULTURE SHOCK

"I was seventeen when I left Tbilisi for the first time to study abroad. I remember the first month was very difficult; I thought all the people around me were bizarre. Culture shock started when my classmate bought a baguette and Coke and just took a bite in front of others without offering it first. Not that I was hungry, I would not have eaten that baguette anyway, but I was shocked to see one person eating and others just watching and talking, as if nothing were wrong.

Another shock came when I went to a party for the first time, all the guests were told they had to bring some food. I did not understand the concept of a party invitation, if the host is not prepared to lay out a spread. The guests were made to distribute plastic plates (it was not even a picnic, we were having a meal at home and they still used plastic!). I was offered some food, which I refused, expecting to be asked again, but the host did not pay further attention and did not come up to me again to insist that I have something to eat. At the end of the party, the guests were made to clean up. I found that very wrong as I expected the hosts would do it on their own. What shocked me most was that, as they left, some visitors took not only their trays and boxes, but also what had remained of the food they brought with them. I refused to take mine back. I thought it rude to give away and then to claim back.

After a few months I settled in and spent a couple of years abroad. When I went back to Georgia, I had another culture shock being back in my homeland. Initially, I found my old friends intrusive and nosy. I had forgotten how friends pop in uninvited and insist on knowing the details of your private life. Once I was talking on the phone while my Georgian friend was waiting patiently as I was speaking. When I hung up she asked: who was that? I wanted to tell her off for being inquisitive and rude, but instead I briefed her about the conversation. I realized she did not mean to interfere; she was just being a Georgian—curious and caring."

Nutsa Tsereteli

chapter five

GEORGIANS AT HOME

HOUSING

There are two factors defining Georgian households: one is money and the other is tradition. In most families, two or three generations live together. Traditionally the youngest son stays with the parents and takes care of them. So, as the house belongs to the youngest, the older ones get some help from the parents to build their own property. Probably the logic behind this arrangement is that while the parents are still working they help the older children to settle down; the youngest son looks after them in their retirement and so he inherits the family house. The girls get only a dowry as their husbands are supposed to provide for them.

These arrangements are not always the case in practice, however. With the economic downturn, not all the older siblings are able to move out by the time the youngest son gets married. And with Georgia becoming more Westernized, many younger sons who have a stable income would rather buy their own property than live with their parents and wait to be given the family home.

So, depending on how rich or how traditional families are, they end up having different housing arrangements. In general young people do not

move out unless they get married or go to live elsewhere—abroad or in a different part of the country. Recently, a Western television journalist was amazed to find out that a Georgian woman minister, with an important seat in the cabinet and a very high salary, still lived with her parents. While showing the journalist her house, she said that as she was single she obviously lived with her parents. However, times are changing in Georgia and an increasing number of young women now choose to live on their own.

People in the cities mainly live in apartments. The gray Soviet style blocks are a familiar sight in every suburb. There are plenty of these "Khrushovkas" in Tbilisi, built during Khrushchev's era. The capital also has some pre-Soviet apartment blocks, however: these are big buildings with beautiful wooden doors, wide windows, high ceilings, and arched balconies. Unlike other places in Georgia, Tbilisi and Batumi also have new developments— terraced houses and apartments built in the past

decade. Most have garages on the first floor, a concierge in the reception, and even a swimming pool on the roof terrace.

Unlike the booming cities, there is very little new construction in rural areas. So the average house in the countryside has to accommodate all the family members. Old-fashioned ways still prevail here, where unemployment is very high and there are no affordable mortgages. If there are two or more married brothers in the family, sometimes all the couples live together with the grooms' parents.

INSIDE A GEORGIAN EXTENDED FAMILY

The Georgian family network includes not only the nuclear family, but also numerous in-laws, relatives, and in-laws' relatives. When a Georgian girl gets married, she moves to the groom's family and lives with his parents. For a man, living with the girl's family is seen as a sign of weakness. Sharing an apartment with the groom's family can create tensions, and new brides often complain to their friends about the old-fashioned ways of the mother-in-law, and of *her* mother-in-law, the groom's grandmother. Live-in in-laws are obviously part of the couple's everyday life. They help to take care of the children and make sure that the young people follow in their ways, which naturally are better and wiser.

Unsurprisingly, more and more young couples in the cities try to get on to the property ladder as soon as possible in order to live independently. For those employed full time, there are plenty of opportunities for affordable mortgages.

It is believed that family life in Georgia should revolve around the head of the family, the man, who is said to be the main decision maker and breadwinner. As a popular saying has it, however, it is the neck that decides where the head looks and what it sees! Georgian men are brought up in a culture that demands they take care of their wives, provide for them, and protect them. But nowadays there are more women employed than men, as they proved to be more flexible after the collapse of the Soviet Union. So it can be quite hard for men who think it shameful to be earning less than their spouses or not to be earning at all.

Even if they're employed full time, Georgian women are still in charge of family life: they supervise their children's homework, instruct those who provide domestic help, and deal with household chores on their own. Georgian men are not at their best at home or in the kitchen. This is changing slowly, but very surely. Grilling on barbecues and making wine in their cellars or garages are generally the only "domestic" activities that men do with joy. At home it is the woman who has to feed, wash, and iron and, in a nutshell, care for the entire family. For Georgian mothers, protecting their family's well-being means pleading with everyone to sit down for a meal at about the same time, forcing their children to eat more, and ensuring that the older generation do not miss their medical appointments and are well looked after.

Athough men rarely live with their in-laws, it is still the wife's mother who is often the butt of Georgian jokes. There are no jokes about the husband's mother, either because it is men who make the jokes, or because, as women live with their in-laws, the tension is too real to joke about.

Most Georgian homes have a prayer corner with icons and candles, though only a few pray regularly. Generally people just cross themselves and say a quick "God have mercy on us" when they pass by a church or see religious symbols.

AN AMERICAN IN BANDZA

Max Schneider, an American volunteer teaching English at the village school of Bandza in Mengrelia, has described life in rural Georgia in his blog:

"Sometimes I see a *mama* (father) riding his daughter to school sitting on the handlebars of his bicycle. Some of you may think that's a dangerous safety hazard (to which a Georgian might reply, what's a safety hazard?), but when you see it in person, it's so damn cute; with the little girl's legs dangling off the front end while the father slowly but proudly weaves his way through the streets of Bandza . . . .

Georgians are steeped in their history, both real and mythical, and most families have photographs of deceased relatives on the walls, very often found along with the icons. Stories of a dead grandparent or uncle pass from one generation to another. "The people on the walls" are always described as the bravest, kindest, and smartest. Georgians have a lively interest in genealogical matters, especially concerning those whom their children wish to befriend or marry. A quick name check is done before giving approval.

RURAL GEORGIA

According to official statistics, 47 percent of Georgia's population live in rural areas (GeoStat, 2009). Life in the countryside follows the rhythm of nature; most people rise at the crack of dawn and go

Speaking of Georgian men . . . I still don't know what a majority of them do . . . . On my way to school every morning, the center is hopping with anywhere from twenty to fifty middle-aged men roaming about, playing *nardi* [backgammon] or cards, and arguing (or discussing politely, depending on your point of view) over anything and everything (to what degree Georgian football stinks, Saakashvili, who's got the bigger gut, etc.). . . . Most of them are town gentlemen out on their morning stroll to . . . nowhere. You can't even get a cup of coffee in Bandza. It's just one big social gathering, like a neighborhood barbershop in Harlem."

to bed soon after the sun sets. Given Georgia's long tradition of agriculture one would assume that people in the country are busy working on their farms and providing for their families. In reality they work hard but earn very little, so migration from the rural areas is very high, especially from the mountainous villages.

Georgian people have strong roots in the regions and always mention where they are from. But the countryside, especially the remote and mountainous areas, seems almost empty: young people have moved to regional towns, and town dwellers have moved to the capital, Tbilisi. In Georgia the nearest town is never too far away, but the situation still creates problems in that sometimes a village will only have one kiosk selling matches, salt, and a few other basic necessities. Life is tough in the remote areas, with poor infrastructure and widespread unemployment. People in the rural areas have fewer opportunities to send their sons and daughters to sports clubs and English classes. Children have long commutes to their schools; sometimes they have to walk thirty to forty minutes every morning.

DAILY SHOPPING

Shopping is part of the daily routine for city dwellers. Even though open-air markets have shrunk in size, shopping for food is never a problem. There are supermarkets, chain grocery stores, corner shops, street sellers, and vegetable carts on every corner of Tbilisi.

A street seller's voice crying, "*Malina, malina*" might wake you up even in the smartest area of the capital. In spring and autumn, people from rural areas come to Tbilisi to sell *malina*, freshly picked berries. The milkman will bring unpasteurized dairy products and yogurt to your doorstep if you ask him to deliver them at certain times. Georgians like buying apples from Gori

(Stalin's birthplace is well-known for the best in the country), watermelons from Central Asia, poultry from local farmers, vegetables from Azeri vendors, potatoes from Greek producers, and cheese from Mengrelian women in the market. In their ideal world, Georgians would receive fresh honey from their relatives in the countryside and make fruit jams or marinade vegetables at home.

Georgians like eating out, especially going to a *sakhiinkle* (house of *khinkali*), where *khinkali*, which are delicious dumplings stuffed with seasoned ham or pork, are served hot with black pepper and cold beer. But there is nothing as mouthwatering as a home-cooked Georgian dinner. Georgians will tell you that foreign products are genetically modified, frozen or precooked meals are bad for your health, and a snack such as a quick sandwich can play havoc with your digestion. They say no to using a microwave. What they prefer is buying fresh bread (*lavash*) from the nearby bakery every day and having it with a traditional, cooked-from-fresh meal. The food is truly delicious, but it is impossible not to notice that they eat too much

cheese and bread and use too much animal fat—
and then complain about high levels of cholesterol.

Gone are the days of standing in line—
everything is available for those who can afford it.
Imported products are still very expensive, however.

GROWING UP IN GEORGIA

The cost of living is lower than in the West, not
only for food but also for domestic help. So, for
most middle-class children, growing up in Georgia
means getting a lot of attention not only from the
family, but also from maids, drivers, and nannies.
Quite often these are older people with university
degrees, who may have lost their jobs at institutions
that ceased to exist after the country achieved
independence (for former teachers of Communist
Party history or engineers at the Soviet plant it is
next to impossible to obtain high-profile jobs).
These rather superior domestic helpers are
encouraged to speak Russian to the children so
that they learn this difficult language with ease.

In most schools in Tbilisi the school day is split
into two sessions: morning classes for secondary
school pupils and afternoon classes for primary.
So children of different ages finish their day at
different times and it is hard for the whole family
to get together for the main meal. If circumstances
permit, however, a late supper (after 9:00 p.m.)
will bring everyone together around the table. If
one of the family members is observing a religious
fast, it is likely that the whole family, except for
small children, will eat vegan food.

Football is the most popular sport among boys,
while more than half of Georgia's girls attend folk

dance classes. At family parties the second-most popular topic (local politics being number one at all times) is discussing the difference between state and private schools, searching for a better tutor of English, piano, or math, and finding out about tennis courts and swimming pools to make sure that one's child goes to the best in town.

Grandparents, along with the domestic help, play a crucial role: when the parents are at work it is they who escort the little talent across town to the best ballet school, sports club, or music academy, wait for them, and bring them home to have a quick dinner before the math tutor knocks on the door.

Childcare

Georgians find it shocking that some people in the West send their toddlers to day care. They believe that till a child turns three or four it is important to keep him or her with a nanny. In an ideal world this would be a family member or a close relative. If there is a need to look outside the family, however, finding a nanny is never a problem, with unemployment very high in the forty to sixty year group.

Nevertheless, most people think that from a couple of years before going to school (at the age of six) children should attend preschools or kindergartens, to prepare them for their new life as pupils. There are plenty of private and state-run kindergartens, so, depending on their

budget, parents can choose between a small family-owned establishment with ten to fifteen children in total or a state center with thirty to forty children in each group.

Georgian parents make sure that their children are well fed and warmly dressed. To outsiders they can sometimes seem to be overfed, overdressed, and overindulged.

EDUCATION
Schools
When it comes to schools, parents who live in the big cities have plenty to choose from. There are all sorts of academic institutions in Tbilisi, Batumi, and Kutaisi, but there are no single-sex schools. For modern Georgians the idea of separating girls and boys seems old-fashioned and even bizarre. And separating children from the family can only be acceptable if the child has special needs or special talents, so only a few schools offer full or half board to their pupils. Tbilisi has international colleges, religious seminaries, and British, American, French, and Spanish schools. With some of the private establishments pupils can spend summer terms in Oxford or Cambridge studying English.

Private schools are a luxury for the few. Ninety percent of Georgians send their children to standard state schools. In rural areas there are only old-fashioned, standard state schools with some of the buildings and staff unchanged from Soviet times. Those who want to continue on to higher education get private tuition to help them prepare for the Unified National Entrance Examinations. Even though the education system has gone through a long and serious reform process, most pupils find it hard to pass this university matriculation test without special after-school coaching.

Maia Charkseliani from the University of Cambridge wrote her Ph.D. thesis on postsecondary education in Georgia. Her research shows that 100 percent of high school graduates in Tbilisi, Batumi, and Kutaisi aspire to enter university, but that rural school graduates and minority groups are seriously underrepresented in higher education. For example, aspiration ratios are only 5 percent in Ninotsminda district (which is mainly populated by the Armenian ethnic minority).

University Life

Georgians say that you can be considered to be part of the intelligentsia if you have three university degrees. It does not, however, merely take a lifetime of passing courses to become an intellectual; it takes three generations. It is your parents' and grandparents' backgrounds that add to your own education and make you a member of the educated elite.

Historically, educating their children was a central value for Georgians. This was reemphasized in Soviet times when education became free and accessible for all. In the 1960s and afterward Georgia had the lowest levels of illiteracy in the USSR and the highest proportion of people with university degrees.

Nowadays, the situation is much the same: young people aspire to higher education and their parents make sacrifices so that their children can join the ranks of the intellectuals. Most universities offer fully funded scholarships for the brightest, while those who do not score high enough have to pay for their education.

Student Financing

Georgians are most generous when it comes to education. It is incomprehensible to Georgian parents that students in Western countries take out loans to finance their studies. In Georgia it is always the parent who sponsors the "child," borrows from the bank, or spends his or her life savings on the "kid's future." If a young person has special talents, then the extended family and friends become involved to make sure that his or her future prospects do not suffer just because the close family is not rich enough to support him.

FASHION AND GROOMING

Looking good is part of daily life and not just for special occasions. Even though it is hard to say what percentage of the family budget is spent on clothes, it's easy to observe that Georgians (especially those with a stable income) invest a lot of time and money in order to look good. Small boutiques, hair salons, and tanning parlors have mushroomed in Tbilisi since the collapse of the USSR. And even though there is one on every corner, they all seem to be busy most of the time. Having their nails done once a week, getting a fake tan, or regularly visiting a salon for a hairdo is very common for Georgian women, especially if they are in their twenties and thirties.

Turkish, Chinese, and Iranian outfits and footwear are sold in open markets, small shops, and on the streets. But they are considered less cool than Western designs. In Tbilisi and Batumi one can always buy the current season's collections from Western designers, but prices are considerably higher. Georgians often joke that it is cheaper to fly to Europe to buy a pair of shoes than to get them in Tbilisi. If luxury brands are beyond your means, you can always find "fake but exactly like the original" Prada shoes, Gucci totes, and D&G clutches.

CONSCRIPTION

Currently all male citizens between the ages of eighteen and twenty-seven are subject to compulsory conscription. Exceptions are made for those with serious health conditions or a disability, or who are enrolled in an institute of higher education. While the rest have to do eighteen months of military service, full-time students are required to spend only a couple of months in the barracks.

After completing the mandatory service, it is possible to enroll in the professional army on a contract, if one is selected. As soldiers' salaries were minimal, this used not to be an option for most graduates. However, the Georgian Special Forces are currently being trained by US partners. Georgia is participating in international peacekeeping missions, and strongly aspires to become a NATO member. So more people are considering a military career, even after graduating from university.

chapter six

TIME OUT

LEISURE

There is a saying in Georgia: "It's good to visit others, but it's better to return home." According to research carried out in 2011, 76 percent of urban and 86 percent of rural dwellers said that home is where they spend most of their free time. Visiting friends and family was the second-most popular answer, yet only 13 percent in the cities and 8 percent in rural areas regularly spent their evenings out and about. Around 2 percent went frequently to pool halls, clubs, bars, theaters, cinemas, bowling alleys, or other places of entertainment.

Even though everyone in Georgia complains about the regional, national, and cable TV channels, watching TV is the most widespread form of relaxation. This is sometimes the only thing that families do together in the evening.

Depending on where one works, office hours as well as holiday time can differ. The national labor code recommends a forty-hour working week and twenty-four days off in a year. Some companies specify how these days can be taken (for example, no more than two weeks at a time), some request that their employees spend only thirty-five hours in the office, while others ignore the code and make their staff do unpaid overtime.

OUT OF DOORS

Whenever possible, most Georgians spend at least
two weeks of their summer vacations at the seaside;
if there is not enough money to go abroad the
Black Sea is not a bad alternative. As the country is
so small, the seaside is never more than a ten-hour
drive from even the most distant areas, and getting
to southwest Georgia (by air, road, or rail) is not a
problem. In summer it is also common to visit
family or relatives in rural areas. Residents of
Tbilisi try to escape the heat and dust of the capital
by going to *dachas*, or summerhouses, in the
surrounding countryside.

In winter almost everyone gets at least a week
off, to be spent in heavy drinking and comparing
which auntie cooks a better *satsivi*, a traditional
New Year's dish. In February and March young
people in the capital go for skiing breaks on the
slopes of Gudauri or Bakuriani, which are within a
three to four hours' drive from Tbilisi. It is firmly
believed that children are healthier if every year

they spend at least two weeks by the seaside in summer and go skiing and sledding for another two weeks in winter. So as people grow up in a culture where it is believed that "a change of air" is important for well-being, they tend to take at least two breaks every year.

Ask your hosts about joining them on a weekend break in Gudauri; they will be more than happy to show you the Georgian slopes, covered with natural snow for more than three months a year. They will most likely tell you that Gudauri and Bakuriani are much better than resorts in Germany, Austria, or Switzerland. This is not necessarily true, but it is worth considering that if you are just a beginner, hiring an instructor and learning how to ski is cheaper in Georgia than anywhere else in Western Europe. And if you are an advanced skier, then you might want to try heli-skiing—skiing in virgin snow is possible only in a small number of countries around the world, so make sure you do not miss the chance.

For those who have the time and money it is possible to go hiking, horse riding across the country, camping, canoeing, rafting, and to enjoy many other outdoor activities.

In his book *Walking in the Caucasus*, Peter Nasmyth states that Georgia has more species of animal and bird than any other European country, and that the country is a walker's paradise, with its diverse climate zones, beautiful landscapes, and stupendous views. However, even though many of the best walks are just a one and a half hours' drive from the capital, more foreigners can be found striding along the paths than locals. Although the paths are well trodden by shepherds, most other Georgians simply wonder why the foreigners bother to walk when one can so easily take a jeep.

FOOTBALL MANIA

Football (soccer) is a religion in Georgia. If you are English or Brazilian, people will immediately ask you about football. The worst thing you could do is tell them that you do not support your local or national team. Every four years, during the World Cup, everything else stops as men and women get together to watch matches on TV. Preparations start early in the morning, as people fill their fridges with stocks of beer and put huge watermelons under the cold tap in the bathroom (there has to be plenty for everyone and there is never enough room for watermelons in the fridge).

The Georgians say that football was born in England, grew up in Brazil, and died in Georgia. They constantly complain about their national team. Even though they have brilliant individual players, Georgia's football team has little to be proud of, so most Georgians support foreign clubs and teams. After you see how much beer is consumed in the course of a single match, you will not find it so surprising that there are so many men with big bellies in Georgia. However, people enjoy playing the game as well as watching it.

Some people jog regularly, go to gyms, and exercise, but what Georgian men like best is to get together once a week and play football. As we have seen, many boys attend football clubs, so when older they like playing the game in the company of friends. Foreigners, especially those who can bring their skills to the team, are welcome to join in. Georgians are not very good at disciplining themselves and exercising, which is probably the reason why playing football is more popular than jogging. Men get together, have fun, joke around, and play. Those who lose buy beer for everyone after the game is over.

TOGETHERNESS

Georgians do not like spending their free time alone. They believe someone has to be depressed to go to a cinema on their own. Only if one were a journalist or a film critic would it be excusable to be eating popcorn alone in the dark. People think that spare time well spent is in the company of friends and family, and the louder it gets the better.

Recent surveys show that Georgians think that what makes their country special is, first of all, its music—songs and dances—and then its cuisine along with its wines. Georgians are at their best when they eat, drink, sing, and dance together.

GEORGIAN CUISINE

Georgian expatriates often joke that a trip to the homeland has to be followed by a very strict diet after returning. Food and wine are probably Georgia's most important attractions; and the cuisine has a lot to offer for vegans and vegetarians. But *mtsvadi* (barbecued pork or beef) and *khinkali* (meat dumplings) are what the locals love most.

Georgian cuisine has absorbed the best culinary traditions of the peoples of the Caucasus, the Middle East, Asia, and the Black Sea coast, though it is the mixture of Turkish, Indian, and Iranian influences, together with Mediterranean cooking traditions, that makes Georgia a destination for food lovers.

The most authentic cold starters include *lobio* (kidney beans with grated walnuts and coriander) and *pkhali* (beets, spinach, or eggplant topped with pomegranate seeds and aromatic herbs).

It is impossible to give a short list of Georgian main courses; one can only say that the cuisine is extremely rich and diverse. With one exception— even though the locals like fish, there is not as great a variety of seafood as there is of meat and poultry. Georgians can cook beef, mutton, pork, chicken, turkey, partridge, and pheasant. They have a variety of different sauces and pastes; depending on the season they use fresh parsley, fennel, mint, basil, and other herbs. However, coriander is ever-present in most dishes all year-round. People of any taste and particular dietary requirements will be able to find their own favorite dish in Georgia. Be prepared for the fact that Georgians often use nuts: adding plenty of hazelnuts and walnuts is a sign of affluence, wealth, and generosity. Nuts are a staple, so there will be no "contains nuts" warnings displayed for your attention.

Do not expect rice or couscous as side dishes. In east Georgia you will be offered *lavashi* (a bread baked on wood), while in west Georgia you will be treated to *gomi* (a cornstarch side dish similar to polenta).

Help yourself to some *tkemali*; this fruit sauce is provided along with salt and pepper at every table. *Tkemali* may steal your heart away from brown HP sauce or ketchup. It is made from the juice of plums, sloes, pomegranates, blackberries, or tomatoes boiled until thick and mixed with spices.

Khinkali and *Khachapuri*

You will hear these two words every time Georgian cuisine is discussed. The dishes come in different variations. Upon leaving, you might be asked by your host if you prefer *khinkali* (giant stuffed dumplings) or *khachapuri* (a filled hot bread cheese dish) and which version was your favourite. So you'll need to try different varieties in order have an answer.

In East Georgia and in the mountainous regions, locals stuff *khinkali* with meat and herbs, cheese, potatoes, salmon, or even garlic. But what

Tbilisi restaurants offer is a simpler variation of this Georgian answer to dumplings. Note that *khinkali* is to be eaten with your hands—"Do not kill it, do not kill it!" people might start shouting if you try to put a fork into your *khinkali*. The truth is that most Georgians, especially young people and women, are unable to eat it without using a fork as *khinkali* is served steaming hot. But the beauty of *khinkali* is the  juice you sip as you bite it. So locals will think highly of you if you manage not to destroy the *khinkali* with a fork and not to waste the sauce.

Keep in mind that if the locals offer you "cheese cake," what they really mean is *khachapuri*—a thin calzone-like dough case filled with mildly salted cheese. In different parts of Georgia cheese is made and seasoned differently. And each area boasts about having the best *khachapuri*. In Tbilisi restaurants you can try them all: Imeruli (*khachapuri* from Imereti), Megruli (a Mingrelian specialty), and Acharuli (*khachapuri* from Achara with eggs and cheese baked in pastry).

GEORGIAN WINE

"[There is] no other country in the world in which wine was so good and drunk so amply as in Georgia."
Sir John Chardin, French-born seventeenth-century traveler

The contemporary Georgian painter Eteri Chkadua says that if she had to choose one symbol of Georgia, it would be wine—the embodiment of hospitality, the Georgian way of life, and traditions. In the picture below she depicts herself with a *kantsi*, the traditional drinking horn.

Made from the horns of rams, goats, oxen, or aurochs, a *kantsi* was cleaned, boiled, polished,

and decorated, creating a unique, durable, and stylish drinking vessel. The modern *kantsi* is a highly valued symbol of Georgia's historic past and is the most common souvenir in the country.

A popular anecdote has it that when the Georgian delegation met Italian diplomats for the first time after the collapse of the USSR, they generously gave them plenty of presents. Apparently, these included nicely wrapped horns, which almost created a diplomatic incident: in many cultures horns are synonymous with cuckoldry. Georgians, however, use them for special toasts. Drinking from a *kantsi* is a real challenge as one cannot put it down and take a rest while drinking. The only way is to down the wine, raise the *kantsi*, and proclaim, "I've downed the wine! Down with our enemies!"

Georgians cannot imagine a meal without wine. Georgian cuisine is backed up by their famous white and red dry wines: "Mukhuzani" with a pleasant, bitter taste; golden, cool "Tetra"; light, straw-colored "Tsinandali" with a sourish, crystal touch; dark, amber-colored, slightly astringent "Teliani"; ruby-colored "Ojaleshi"; the mildly sweet, emerald-like, sparkling "Manavi"; garnet-red, honey-tasting "Kindzmarauli"; dark, ruby-colored, velvety "Khvanchkara"; light-green "Gurjaani"; dark, golden, fruity "Tibaani"; and a host of others.

THE BEGINNINGS OF WINE

"Wine's name itself is of Georgian origin, *gvino*, and October, harvest month, is named Gvinobistve (the month of wine). Mosaics attest to the influence of the Georgian wine god Aguna. The cult of grapevine and wine forms part of the Georgian psyche—present from spiritual and religious symbolism to the more earthbound aspects of life. In the first part of the fourth century St. Nino arrived in Georgia bringing the word of Christianity with an upheld cross made in the shape of an intertwined grapevine arbour. Georgians venerate the vine and its product, and wherever wine is served, a toast is voiced and big-hearted, misty-eyed oratory issues forth. Wine as evidenced from the Georgian folklore and history is used for solemn or mournful ritual, in copious quantities and rarely, if ever, diluted."

Robert Parsons

In Georgia's very macho culture, foreigners are plied with wine. Note that getting drunk before others is seen as a sign of weakness. For those who are used to sipping wine rather than draining a full glass or *kantsi*, this can have serious consequences. This is how Wendell Steavenson describes her experience of drinking with the Georgians in her book, *Stories I Stole from Georgia*:

"It was a kind of aggression. When they did not know you well, they filled your glass and filled it again and carefully watched how you drank it. This was their measure of you; this was done to disarm you . . . The quantities, however, were still very large and could provoke either love or violence. This was the Georgian way, friend or enemy with nothing in between. History was lost in tradition, drinking a way of remembering and forgetting at the same time."

THE *SUPRA*

While eating and drinking is a central part of any gathering in Georgia, the *supra* is more than *khinkali*, *khachapuri,* or the best of Georgian cuisine. As we have seen, it is a feast that combines a generous table with plenty of food and wine, welcoming hosts, a toastmaster, guitar music, and tipsy guests singing *supruli*—Georgian party songs.

EATING OUT

Modern Georgians like dining out. There are all sorts of restaurants offering local specialties served as *mezes*, a selection of small dishes). At one end of the spectrum there are small, inexpensive, informal places with no menus in English (or no menus at all). As people inquire about the "soup of the day" or the "chef's special" in the West, Georgians talk to waiters to find out "what is fresh" and order it.

In very informal places, the check could be a waiter's scribble or even a verbal statement. However, as foreigners might be overcharged, it is important to establish the prices before making orders.

In an expensive restaurant, you are more likely to have a proper menu and a printed check, and will be able to pay by card. These are mainly high-class restaurants serving Georgian, Russian, Thai, Chinese, Indian, Italian, or French food.

If you are not a smoker it is worth finding a far corner in the restaurant (do not wait to be seated, just find a place you like). There are no specially designated smoking areas and most people smoke while others are eating around the same table. The attitude toward smoking in Georgia is the same as it was twenty years ago in the West. So, if you object to passive smoking, you have to make it clear to others, otherwise they will assume that you are fine with it.

TIPPING

Generosity is very important to Georgians and being cheap or economical never reflects well on you. So just round up the check and do not take any change the waiter brings back to the table unless it is in notes. This is what most locals do (and the same rule applies in taxis). People might expect foreign guests to tip up to 5 percent in cash, though it won't be a problem if you simply round up the check. Just make sure that you are not seen counting coins in Georgia.

FOLK AND POLYPHONIC MUSIC

A Taste of Eternity

"Everything in Georgia sings—the people, the mountains, the rivers, the sky and the earth . . . They sing about war and peace, love, their homes . . . They sing about their mothers, sweethearts, friends, and brothers . . . Georgian song is remarkably beautiful—happy and sad, strong and gentle. There is no other polyphony like it. It is overwhelming and refined. Hearing it just once will give you a taste of eternity."

Mstislav Rostropovich

Archaeological findings and written sources show that Georgian musical culture is about three thousand years old. According to ancient sources (the Assyrian King Sargon in the eighth century BCE and Xenophon, the Greek historian in the fourth century BCE), Georgians had songs to cheer themselves during work, as well as war songs and dances, where one performer would start and others would join in.

Although surrounded by homophonic countries, whose musical traditions are characterized by a single melodic line with accompaniment, Georgia developed a rich and unique polyphonic musical culture. Most Georgian folk and church songs have two or more independent melodic parts sounding together. Tamta Turmanidze, leader of the London-based Maspindzeli Choir, points out that dissonant chords, very common in Georgian singing, may initially sound strange to Western ears, but that after a while most Westerners find the combination of separate but harmonizing melodies magical. "Georgian folk music is predominantly vocal with an amazing diversity of polyphonic forms, regional styles, and musical dialects. Songs with three voices are the most common. Traditionally, the higher voices are sung by two soloists and the bass more often by several singers. Georgian secular and pagan magical music is sung by singers of the same gender. However, sometimes mixed women's, men's, and children's performances take place in ritual circular dances and in some forms of family performance. Song structure varies from region to region. Rhythmic improvisational trio songs are common in the western provinces. Songs from the mountainous regions of Svaneti and Rach'a are often accompanied by traditional dances."

"CHAKRULO"

In 2001, UNESCO proclaimed Georgian Polyphonic Singing a "Masterpiece of the Oral and Intangible Heritage of Humanity." Well before that, though, when Georgia was still part of the USSR, one particular Georgian song travelled beyond the Iron Curtain and much further.

In 1977 NASA launched two unmanned spacecraft, Voyager 1 and Voyager 2, to study Jupiter and Saturn. The probes continued into the outer solar system to gather data about its gas giants, about which little was known. Voyager 1, currently the farthest human-made object from the Earth, is carrying a Golden Record that includes "Chakrulo," a patriotic folk song from Kakhetia.

GEORGIAN DANCE

Every region of Georgia has its own musical tradition and style of performance. Some Georgian dances have an oriental style, others have no trace of this. They may be based on traditional stories.

In most Georgian dance styles, the woman glides elegantly in her colorful costume. The man keeps his upper body very still, showing off his skillfull footwork. Couples are flirtatious with one another, but the man is always respectful toward the woman. The man does not touch the woman—he tries to get closer, but the woman distances herself, gliding gracefully away.

Stories Told Through Dances

If you know the stories they tell, it is even more inspiring to watch these folk dances on stage or on the screen, and they will tell you a great deal about the Georgian people.

A quintessentially Georgian dance is "Khevsuruli." This mountain dance embodies the Georgian spirit. It unites love, chivalry, and respect for women, competition, beauty, and courage. The dance starts out with a flirting couple. Unexpectedly, another young man appears, also seeking the hand of the woman. An argument breaks out and soon turns into a vigorous fight between the two men, who are then joined by their supporters. The young men from both sides attack each other with swords and shields. While they are dancing one man has to fight off three attackers. However, when the tension reaches its climax, the girl reappears, looking for her beloved. According to tradition, when a female throws down her headdress, the men must stop fighting. So the girl gracefully dances her way to the middle and puts her white silk scarf amidst the men. They freeze and the dance stops abruptly.

CINEMA AND THEATER

Tbilisi has about a dozen cinemas and most young people go to the movies at least twice a month. Outside the capital most cinemas show only one movie a week, so, with not much else to do, watching one movie every seven days is almost a must for young locals. After the August war in 2008, some cinemas decided not to show foreign movies dubbed in Russian. As there was not a large enough budget for Georgian dubbing, some now show Hollywood films with Georgian subtitles. So there is a lot on offer for English speakers, but you have to make inquiries in advance as some cinemas still show the Russian versions.

In the past Georgia made major contributions to Soviet cinema, but the movie industry collapsed with the USSR and came back to life only recently, after twenty years.

Unlike the cinema, the theater has thrived even during the worst times. Surprisingly, during economic downturns tickets sell out weeks in advance for premières. For non-Georgian speakers the best place to go is Gabriadze Marionette Theater, founded and run by the celebrated Soviet screenwriter and theater director Rezo Gabriadze. He once said that he laughs when people say that the theater is in crisis "because theater thrives on crisis." In his tiny theater, which seats one hundred people, on a stage only a little bigger than a dining table, Gabriadze proves his point.

IN TBILISI

Tbilisi has a lot to offer the visitor. There is information about sightseeing at the Tourism Office on the south side of Freedom Square. Walking through the old city, with its ornamented, overhanging balconies and cobbled streets, is probably the most authentic introduction to the culture. One can spend hours wandering around ancient churches, winding streets, charming shops, and elegant restaurants.

Two of the most important religious structures in the city are the Sioni Cathedral and the Anchiskhati Basilica, built in the fifth and sixth centuries respectively. Anchiskhati Basilica is just a couple of minutes' walk from the Marionette Theater and the arty Sans Souci café, decorated by Revaz Gabriadze. It's worth stopping off at this attractive little café with its view of the Basilica.

Some of the splendor of Tbilisi can be seen along Rustaveli Avenue, where fine architecture and brand-name stores line up with government buildings and galleries. Such attractions as the Tbilisi History Museum are worth visiting to get a better feel of the city's past and present.

For the young and fit who have remembered to bring their hiking shoes, a genuine adventure awaits up the hills of the city. Just hike over to the Narikala Fortress and the Mother of Georgia Monument; even though the paths are greatly eroded in parts, once you reach the top you will be rewarded with breathtaking views.

High on the Elia Hill, opposite Narikala, rises the Tsminda Sameba (Holy Trinity) Cathedral, consecrated in 2004 after a decade of building

work. A massive expression of traditional
Georgian architectural forms in concrete, brick,
granite, and marble, it measures 276 feet (84 m) to
the top of the gold-covered cross above its central
dome. The Sameba Cathedral is the third-tallest
Eastern Orthodox Cathedral in the world. The
huge dome creates a larger and much brighter
central space than you'll find in most Georgian
churches. A large-scale, new illuminated
manuscript of the New Testament, in a jewel-
studded silver cover, stands in a glass case to the
right of the altar.

Abanotubani—the Tbilisi Baths
Tbilisi is famous for Abanotubani, the Turkish
baths district, which is within walking distance
of the city's most modern, lively, and Westernized
spot, Shardeni Street, where the best restaurants
and bars have mushroomed over the last decade.
After a heavy night of drinking there is nothing
better than a glass of Borjomi—the local mineral
water—and a sulfur bath to recover from a
hangover. This is something locals do with joy

and would recommend to any foreigner. It is absolutely worth following their advice.

Georgians love visiting bathhouses with their friends. In the past, baths were everybody's favorite meeting place; there the citizens would gather and exchange information in the days before there were newspapers. Future mothers-in-law would take their sons' fiancées to the baths to steal a glimpse of them, while the men cured their hangovers in the gents' section. It was even rumored that the famous sulfur waters could cure impotence. This exaggeration, or desire to promote Tbilisi, brought a disaster to the Georgian capital. Agha Mohammad Khan, the ruler of Persia at the end of the eighteenth century, seized the city and headed immediately to Abanotubani, to bathe. When he realized the waters had failed to work their magic, he vented his frustration on the entire city, razing it to the ground. Today, Abanotubani is one of the first places to show to visitors. Sulfur waters definitely do not cure impotence, but do give a shine to one's hair and skin; taking a deep, hot bath is the best relaxation for a Georgian.

OUTSIDE THE CAPITAL

When the weather is good, Georgians like getting out of Tbilisi. There is plenty to do and see. The locals will insist you visit the ancient capital of Georgia, Mtskheta: walk around the eleventh-century Svetitskhoveli Cathedral and admire the beautiful view from the sixth-century Jvari Church. Sample the *khinkali* at the famous Salobie restaurant on the road out of Mtskheta. This is exactly what the Tbilisi dwellers do on weekends.

Georgian children visit churches and historic sites on school trips. One of the most popular destinations is the cave city of Vardzia, a monastery dug into the mountainside in southern Georgia.

A weekend trip to Signagi is very popular among young couples. This East Georgian town, with its small churches and walk-in wedding bureau open day and night, is the most romantic destination in the country.

If they have long holidays, Georgians travel further afield. In the past not many people went to the mountains because the journey was long and uncomfortable. But recently the roads have been rebuilt and there are daily helicopter flights from Tbilisi. So Georgians have rushed to explore the mountains of Svaneti, Tusheti, and Khevsureti, where lifestyle, traditions, and customs have not changed much for centuries. In summer, Svaneti is full of Georgian and foreign tourists admiring the medieval villages with their centuries-old tower houses peppered among the gigantic mountains.

SOME "MUST-SEE" TOURIST DESTINATIONS

The Borjomi-Kharagauli National Park in central Georgia covers more than 210,000 acres (85,000 ha) of native forest and is home to rare species of flora and fauna.

Davit Gareja Monastery, set in parched countryside in the Kakheti region of east Georgia includes hundreds of cells, churches, chapels, refectories, and living quarters hollowed out of the rock face.

In the north of the country, Mount Kazbeg is where the Georgians believe Prometheus was chained for stealing fire from the gods. Visit the scenic town of Stephantsminda with the fourteenth-century Sameba ("Trinity") Church on the mountain's snowy peak.

To all Georgians, Gori is synonymous with one man: this is the town where Iosif Jughashvili—later Joseph Stalin—was born and went to school. You can visit it in a day trip from Tbilisi.

The seaside city of Batumi is the capital of the autonomous republic of Achara in southwestern Georgia. It's the country's second capital, the biggest city after Tbilisi, and an important port and commercial center.

We've seen that Georgians love spending summers by the Black Sea. Accommodation prices in Achara vary from US $10 up to US $200 a night, so there is something for every budget. Batumi is a bit more expensive than the surrounding areas, but it has more to offer as well. Recently it has become a destination for Armenian and Iranian tourists.

Batumi is very quirky and eclectic. Some streets remind one of Turkey, with colorful open bazaars. There are breezy seaside cafés, grand nineteenth-century buildings, and gray Soviet-era apartment blocks. It is a cluttered, cozy place with a long, open seaside promenade.

Katie Melua's Sweet Memories

"My parents are from Batumi, so for me it is a city with a special charm and magic. I was very little when my family moved to the UK, but we have been visiting Georgia almost every year since then. The best memories of my childhood are associated with summer holidays and the fun we used to have during our trips to truly breathtakingly beautiful places. We would arrive in Tbilisi and drive to Batumi, and even though it took half a day, I absolutely loved the ritual. I had something to look forward to, half way through, in Rikoti Gorge. Then we'd stop by a roadside café to find a wooden table under the shade of big trees by the river and have the most delicious *mtsvadi*, meat barbeque, that the locals make right there, in front of you. We would rest and continue our journey through the beautiful green scenery. Just remembering those days fills me with tranquillity and peace.

Apart from swimming, sunbathing, and playing cards on the beach, the Black Sea has its own seaside rituals. There are old women selling freshly boiled, steaming hot corn. They are mouthwateringly moist; you put some salt on top and bite as you watch the sunset. But what I loved most was eating sunflower seeds on the beach. In the West they are sold peeled and packed, this kind of kills the ritual. In Georgia you shell each tiny, black, fried-in-salt sunflower seed as you talk and eat them one after the other. It is so addictive sometimes that it's impossible to stop.

Often we would go to have picnics by the waterfalls near Batumi. Take a big watermelon with you, put it under the waterfall to cool, and eat it in the open. It's truly heavenly."

chapter seven

TRAVEL, HEALTH, & SAFETY

Georgia is a small country and there is a greater reliance on road travel than is usual elsewhere. It has a reasonable rail infrastructure, and there are several internal flights, although these are not very popular or very reliable. The past decade has seen considerable improvements to both the road and the rail networks. Traveling around Georgia, however, is still a necessity rather than a pleasure. Drivers have to put up with poorly maintained roads in some areas, and with reckless fellow drivers everywhere. Even so, the splendid landscapes on the way to some stunning destinations make driving an option well worth considering.

WELCOME TO TBILISI

Most departures from Tbilisi International Airport take place at the crack of dawn, and most arrivals land in TBS well after midnight. Foreign citizens, including Russian nationals, are given a visa at the airport. There it is possible to withdraw cash from ATM machines or exchange money 24/7 at a small kiosk. Dollars are useful but it is best to have the local currency, Georgian Lari (GEL). Even though most official Web sites say that the airport is connected to the city by a modern railway, this is not

yet fully completed and it is better to take a taxi. As
you leave the terminal building, you will see a stand
of licensed taxis with a fixed fare to the city center.

It is not difficult to find accommodation in
Tbilisi; there are plenty of variously priced hotels
as well as apartments and rooms to rent. However,
there are not many short-let apartments. Most
people will only agree to tenancy if they can let it
for a couple of months rather than a few days.

If you are looking for a hotel or just a room with
a family, there is a wide selection. And if you are
ready to make Tbilisi your new home, and need an
apartment or a house for at least a year, there is
even more choice. Many families who were wealthy
during Soviet times are now unable to make ends
meet. Some let their property and move out of the
capital, so for the amount of money you could
expect to pay for a studio apartment in central
London or New York, you can get a huge
apartment with leather sofas, semiprecious
Czech chandeliers, oil paintings on the walls,
and ornamental vases on the window sills.

GETTING AROUND TOWN

In his book *Young Stalin*, Simon Sebag Montefiore calls Tbilisi "the intimate city." He says "Tiflis was—and still is—a languid town of strollers and boulevardiers who frequently stop to drink wine at the many open-air taverns: if the showy, excitable Georgians resemble any other European people, it is the Italians." Walking along Rustaveli Avenue can be a real joy; it represents Georgia's love of education, culture, theater, opera, elegance, and chic. Those who live in or come to visit Tbilisi take evening strolls along Shardeni Street, Rike Park, or around Lisi Lake.

Only 7 percent of the Georgian population walk to work on a daily basis, however; most of these live in rural areas. Tbilisians like strolling at leisure, but walking to work is almost impossible in the capital. There are several main streets with broad and clean pedestrian paths. But as soon as you leave the center, you might come across a gas station or a café right in the middle of the sidewalk, and there's no way of avoiding them.

The Metro is the cheapest form of transportation in Tbilisi, but not many middle-class people use it. There are only two lines and it is fairly easy to get from A to B, so you should have no trouble finding your way around. However, you might be the only foreigner in the carriage. The same applies to buses. Ten percent of rural dwellers and 20 percent of Tbilisians get on a bus for their daily commute in the morning. Public transportation is not fashionable, so people with stable jobs, especially the younger generation, tend to avoid the Metro and buses for their daily commute.

The locals find so-called *marshutkas*—yellow minivans that drive around the center— more comfortable. You can easily catch one, travel, and pay a fixed fee just before you get off. There are dozens of different *marshutka* lines, though the logic of their routes is not easy to fathom and there is no Web site that has detailed information. So, unless your host tells you which one you need to catch, don't play the guessing game and lose your way. In case you do get lost, keep your hotel or house address written down on a piece of paper in Georgian. Show it to people in the street, and even if you do not have any language in common they will do their best to help. Few Georgians would leave a foreigner in need in the street. Apart from anything else, they are too curious and friendly to ignore you.

Fifty percent of Tbilisi people use either their own cars or taxis every day. There is no congestion charge and most Georgian cities are full of cheap secondhand cars from Europe. Middle-income people are able to afford cars and traffic jams are becoming the norm, especially in Tbilisi. The taxi service is not very expensive; you can drive from

one part of the capital to the opposite and pay the equivalent of a single bus fare in London, though this works only if you book a taxi through your hotel reception and get a quote in advance. As we have seen, tipping takes the form of rounding up the fare. Hailing a cab on the street is not a good idea for foreigners, unless you want to pay double.

TRAVEL AROUND THE COUNTRY

There are various options for traveling outside the capital: a helicopter, if you want to visit Svaneti or Tusheti in the Georgian mountains; a night train, if you would like to see the neighboring capitals of Baku or Erevan, or Batumi and Poti in west

Georgia; or bus, if you want to go to any city or town within the country. Or a *marshutka*, for a more comfortable and quick drive plus the opportunity to get off where you want to rather than at the designated bus

stops. You could also hire a taxi, which would cost a bit more but the driver would be with you for as many days as you want him. Last but not least, you could ask a friend or someone you know to give you a lift and offer to fill their tank with gas.

As one Georgian says, she has never been to Svaneti but she has been to the heliport departure terminal three times. Because driving to Svaneti takes almost a day, many people opt for the one-hour helicopter flight, but depending on the weather conditions it can be canceled at very short notice. So beware.

Travel by *marshutka* can be erratic as well. The drivers are more flexible, so you can ask them to depart from their route to reach a specific destination. But you need to keep in mind that they do not have fixed timetables. Having identified the correct *marshutka* departure point (they are different for east and west Georgia, so you will need to ask), gone there, found the right *marshutka*, spoken to the driver, and told him if you need to be taken somewhere specific, you then wait for other people to show up. The *marshutka* will not depart unless it is full. So it's hard to plan. It's also hard to travel alone if you do not speak any Georgian or Russian, as it is unlikely that the driver will speak English. You can always rely on the help of friendly Georgians, who will introduce themselves, translate for you, or offer you their food and drink. But if there are no young people present who can speak English, you will have to make a choice and decide whether you really want to save money or whether you'd rather take a taxi with a guide/driver who is ready to spend a day or two with you.

On the road, strangers are generally quiet; they have brief conversations, but not too long or too loud. If you are traveling with a big group, you will need to have your earplugs ready. They will joke, laugh, and ignore their fellow passengers. If this group starts talking about politics and if people happen to have different ideas, earplugs will be of no use.

Inconvenienced

It is better not to go into any public toilets. They are everyone's, so no one cleans them properly. Try to find a decent roadside café; they have relatively clean toilets. Even so, relatively clean with a squat toilet ("Turkish" as the locals call them) is the best you can hope for. Now that Georgia is booming, new roads are being built and old ones are being improved, so it is becoming quicker and easier to travel within the country. However, even though there are developments in many areas, the hole in the ground covered with a porcelain stand is still very common. One appalled American traveler even blogged that the USA should not give any more money to Georgia until the Turkish toilets were replaced with Western ones. (She later conceded that it just takes a bit of time to get used to them.)

GEORGIAN DRIVING

You will notice that there are beauty parlors on every Tbilisi street corner. As you leave the capital, you will see fewer salons for women but many more for men and their toys. Car washes are everywhere and they are never empty.

The Georgian attitude to cars, and the way people drive, amazed American teacher Max Schneider. He found it difficult to understand why Georgian men spend so much time cleaning their cars, why they keep an extra liter of gasoline in an old plastic beer bottle somewhere in their car;

"why they park where they park (which is pretty much wherever they want). . . . Or, what about when they drive with their kids in their laps Britney Spears style."

CAR RENTAL

If you still want to drive in Georgia, there are international as well as local car rental services in Tbilisi. There may not be a great choice of vehicles, but the demand is also not high, so you are likely to find a suitable car. Carrying official documents is a general legal requirement in Georgia, and you will need to present a valid driver's licence as well as your passport at the rental office. There, you will find yourself in a circle of other foreigners. If Georgians need a car, they just ask around and borrow one for a day or two; filling out the papers to rent a car is a truly touristic experience exclusive to foreigners.

HEALTH

There are no particular health hazards in Georgia. You do not need any vaccinations before entering the country and need not be afraid of catching any endemic diseases.

There is a national health service that is largely free for the locals, but the system is inefficient and needs to be reformed. Most Georgians also have health insurance. What they do when they have a serious health issue is make a phone call. They ask around and find out who's the best cardiologist, say, or the best pediatrician. Then they call the doctor's cell phone and visit him or her either at the clinic during working hours or at home if it is urgent. If for any reason you need to see a doctor, you should do likewise. If you need a receipt from the doctor in order to claim insurance after you get back to your country, it's worth checking in advance to see if the doctor is able to give you one.

SAFETY

Most areas of Georgia are safe and crime rates are no higher than in the West. There is limited access to Abkhazia and South Ossetia, the borders of which are controlled by peacekeeping forces. You would need a special permit to go to the disputed territories. Most foreigners find the road network confusing and poorly maintained, and "Georgian driving" alarming, but no major precautions need be taken when traveling around the country.

The reforms introduced since the 2003 Rose Revolution have had a considerable effect. Some reforms were more controversial than others, and almost all were met with some resistance and criticism. But one thing that Georgians are unanimous about is their pride in the new police force. In 2005 the old, corrupt, and disrespected militiamen were replaced by the Patrol Police. There have been a few cases of misconduct by the Patrol Police, but these are exceptions rather than the norm. The speed limit is 37 mph (60 kmph) in cities and 50 mph (80 kmph) out of town. In the past, very few Georgians obeyed the speed limits, used seat belts, or did not drive drunk. However, now the Patrol Police strictly monitor the situation on the roads and most Georgians grudgingly put on their seat belts as soon as they get into their cars. The police respond to emergency calls very quickly and are there within minutes if you have an accident. So Georgian roads have become considerably safer in less than a decade.

This is true about the general situation in the country as well. Some Georgians leave their houses and cars unlocked. Violent crimes involving foreigners are rare, but it's still worth following some basic safety rules, such as not walking alone in the poorly lit outskirts after midnight and not carrying all your cash with you.

Georgians are very liberal when it comes to female fashion; you will see a lot of girls with miniskirts and deep cleavages almost everywhere. You are free to dress as you wish in most places. You cannot, however, enter an Orthodox church wearing shorts or a strapless top. In some mountain areas there are even different paths for men and women, and it is not advisable to show up there without a local guide or someone who can meet you and inform you about the customs.

chapter eight

BUSINESS BRIEFING

BUSINESS CULTURE AND ENVIRONMENT

You will be surprised to find that everyone seems to be related to, or acquainted with, each other in Georgia. It is a very small country and people in the capital either know each other or know somebody who knows them. This often creates problems for employers who believe in equal opportunities and fair selection, rather than in offering jobs to friends of friends.

A British manager based in Georgia said it took him some time to realize that 75 percent of the staff were either related or had met each other before joining the company. "It explains why some people are so confident at job interviews. One person we recruited recently turned out to have very little experience, but at the interview she came across as very competent; now I realize she just knew what we would be asking her," he said. He was also surprised that news travels so quickly in Tbilisi. "You tell one colleague that you are planning to go to France for your holidays and the next day everyone in the office is wishing you "bon voyage."

According to a Georgian joke, "You are Georgian if your uncle is a minister." It is worth remembering that when Georgians refer to their "sisters" or "brothers," sometimes they might have cousins or in-laws in mind. And when Georgians say "my cousin" they might mean their third cousin twice removed or a remote relative. The same is true for aunts and uncles, so almost everyone has at least one uncle in the government.

Doing Business in Georgia

In 2011, a World Bank report ranked Georgia 12th out of 183 economies. Significant improvements related to two indicators: obtaining credit and greater access to corporate information during legal proceedings. The report found Georgia to be one of the most open countries to foreign investment. In terms of economic freedom Georgia is ranked 15th out of 43 countries in the Europe region, and

its overall score is higher than the world average. In the 2011 Index of Economic Freedom the Georgian economy maintained its status as a "mostly free" economy. Reforms in business freedom, trade freedom, fiscal freedom, and labor freedom have stimulated economic development.

Corruption

In this strongly relationship-based society, it is extremely important who you know and who they can put you in touch with, but gone are the Soviet days when you had to bribe the secretary with a box of chocolates or perfume in order to pass your messages on to her boss. Petty corruption has been almost eradicated in the past five years. You no longer need to hand over an envelope with cash to the clerk to register a company or get some paperwork done, though it is too early to say that Georgia has managed to wipe out corruption completely.

However, there is more to running a business in Georgia than getting your company registered quickly and efficiently. Stephan Fitch is an American businessman who has been doing business in Tbilisi for many years. Married to a Georgian, he knows the country and its culture. He says it took him some time to realize that Georgians do not fully share the Western sense of fair play: "In the '90s I saw a lot of Europeans doing business in Tbilisi and I observed how mistakes were made and how wide the perception gap was. Europeans and Americans blamed things on corruption . . . in reality it was the arrogance of Westerners and their ignorance of Georgians. The Eastern trading mentality has existed in Georgia for centuries and for those who come to this country it is important to understand that the locals will not lose an opportunity to gain a trading advantage."

Business Gifts vs Bribes
In general business gifts are not common and are usually limited to souvenirs, books, and corporate or promotional DVDs. Expensive items are rarely given or expected. There are exceptions, of course, and the spirit with which these are given should be considered with care. Some things, however, that in Western culture might be seen as a bribe, in a Georgian context are just sincere gifts.

If you want to avoid an awkward situation do not ask your Georgian office representative or business partner to tell you where to buy a present for your wife; they might just get it for you. Georgians do not say openly if they need something, so people are used to reading between the lines and hearing more than is said. If you are not careful, "Where can I get a bottle of good Georgian wine?" can be heard as "Please buy me a bottle to take home." People think it's very important to reciprocate, so if you have brought some presents and distributed them on your arrival, they will do their best not to lose face and so give something in return before you leave.

MEETINGS: FORMAL AND INFORMAL

In a recent survey, 90 percent of Georgians admitted to having been late for a meeting at least once. More than half said that they happen to be delayed fairly regularly. Not only do meetings generally start later than planned, they carry on for longer than anticipated. This is because it is likely that you will be asked to join an informal meeting, a lunch or a dinner, right after the formal one has ended.

NEVER APOLOGIZE, NEVER EXPLAIN
If you are Georgian and you are late for a meeting you need to go into the room with a very serious face. You do not excuse yourself or say things like "I've been stuck on public transportation." You just make sure that your face says, "I've just come from another meeting that was more important than this one."

Like the country's food and traditions, the Georgian meeting style reflects many cultural influences. Nick Shurgaia, a businessman who has worked in Britain and former Soviet countries as well as in his native Georgia, says that individualism, high energy, natural warmth, and boisterousness are its distinguishing features. He thinks that hospitality has influenced business culture because pleasing the guest is considered to be an honor for the host.

People need to get to know each other, to drink a little bit to bring down barriers and to build relationships. Perhaps trust develops when you break bread together. Stephan Fitch has often been asked to continue an important conversation in a nearby restaurant. He says that most Westerners find Georgian kindness overwhelming, but they are genuine in their desire to please and entertain their foreign partners. Georgians think it very important to make friends with a possible partner and not just to sit within four walls and discuss the bottom line. Even so, there are cultural pitfalls, and he has the following advice for anyone planning a business trip to Tbilisi.

CLEAR COMMUNICATION

"Perceptions of the Westerners are as skewed as yours of them. And you have to sit and listen and observe and understand their approach in order to calibrate your vision to them. I work with people who are fluent in English, but it is still their second language and the simplest of phrases or colloquial language can cause problems. Sometimes they do not quite grasp what the assignment is, but they are too proud to show this. They will nod and you will think they understand you, but months later you might discover that they misunderstood what you said when they promised to deliver; this might put your business back to square one. I get upset with friends there: you just want to pull your hair out sometimes when you realize that they gave you the impression they understood what you meant and they got it completely wrong."

Stephan Fitch

WOMEN IN BUSINESS AND POLITICS

Western businesswomen may be surprised when local partners offer to carry their briefcase, hold their laptop, or say "After you" while opening doors. Gallantry and chivalry are more important than business protocol. Your Georgian counterpart might inquire about your marital status; and ask if you have children and who takes care of them while you are on a business trip. Even on your first meeting with senior people, you should expect more than a formal exchange of pleasantries.

If you are meeting a local female counterpart, a politician or a businesswoman, it is important to look good. It's most likely that she will be dressed in a designer outfit and would have come to the office straight from the beauty parlor.

PRESENTATIONS

Georgians will be impressed if you make a colorful
and elaborate presentation. Less so if you go into
too much detail at the very first meeting. Try to
keep your presentation under thirty minutes, with
time for questions afterward. As the devil is in the
detail, you will clearly have to spell things out at
some point. But at this stage your audience will not
be interested in the follow-up.

NEGOTIATIONS

As one Westerner put it, Georgians assume that
you are cunning and that they should be cunning
and that the two of you should meet and figure out
the common ground. So do not put all your cards
on the table. The Georgians will put on a cool front
in negotiations. However, even when bargaining
and asking for more they will still be prepared to
settle for less.

You might be interrupted by phone calls and
"urgent matters." For Georgians it is important to
give the impression that they are busy and their time
cannot be wasted discussing petty concerns. They
will try to agree on general principles first and look
at the project details and deadlines afterward. It is
likely that they will agree to a schedule but after
signing the contract will ask to extend the deadlines.

If you are a middleman offering services, they
may say they need more time to make a decision,
and then try to cut you out and approach the
service provider directly while you are waiting to
hear back from them.

Your Georgian counterparts will try to gain the
upper hand if they sense any weakness on your

part. Whether you are offering it or accepting it yourself, "compromise" sounds like "surrender" to Georgians. Just replace it with the word "consensus," which sounds better to their ears.

If, in the course of negotiating, you offer an extra incentive that they are not interested in, they will think it too rude to say bluntly that your offer does not interest them. They will thank you politely and not bring the matter up again. Georgians find it hard to say no; they would rather ignore your proposal than say, "Thanks, but this is not something we would consider at this moment."

FRESH OUT OF SCHOOL

One British businessman said that when he first entered the State Chancellery in Tbilisi, he thought that the people he saw in the corridors were students on work experience. He discovered that they were either ministers or deputy ministers. President Saakashvili was thirty-seven when he was elected in 2004. Since then most people with ministerial portfolios have been in their thirties, a few of them in their late twenties.

PROMISES AND REALITY: TWO VIEWS

Nick Shurgaia and Stephan Fitch know Georgian business culture inside out. Nick Shurgaia says that Georgians are natural optimists, which often results in a divergence between promises and reality. But international exposure is making them more aware of how business is done elsewhere. He has this advice for businesspeople looking for opportunities in Georgia:

"I say I believe that the most extensive promises are made out of good intentions rather than deception. History has taught Georgians to focus on the better side of things, see possibilities rather than dangers and difficulties. And the Soviet past has contributed toward the lack of discipline. The reality is that good intentions and willingness to make a quick buck often prevail over realistic assessments. On the positive side, the Georgian business community is increasingly exposed to best international practices and many businesspeople care genuinely about their reputation and brand. So old approaches are being replaced with more sophisticated work relationships."

Stephan Fitch agrees in a way, but says that the business culture is changing very slowly. Many Georgians who study in the West go back to their country without any hands-on Western experience. The Georgian government eagerly employs graduates of European and American business schools, and some of them know just enough to be dangerous: they think they fully understand how Western systems work but they only have a "classroom or textbook knowledge."

"But on the positive side Georgian people are genuinely keen to move ahead. They are by far the most entrepreneurial people in the region. They are eager, they are quick on their feet, they see opportunity and they go after it, and they are quick learners. The overall perception I have had of the country is definitely positive. It has its own problems, but I am willing to put that into the equation when I am doing business there. As the end of the day it's risk/reward and if you are not willing to accept the risks you are not going to get the rewards."

CONTRACTS

When drawing up a contract it would be wise to use the services of a qualified bilingual lawyer, not only to avoid any misunderstanding, but also to keep abreast of the changing legal regulations.

RULES ARE MADE TO BE CIRCUMVENTED

Most Georgians think that rules can be questioned, rewritten, and improved, and red lines are a recommendation. So they try to find ways around things all the time. Once a senior French official made a recommendation to a Georgian minister about reforming a certain sector. The minister said that he thought the idea was great, but it came into conflict with a clause of the Georgian constitution. However, the Georgian minister promised to talk to his friends in parliament and see if it was possible to have the clause changed. The Frenchman was absolutely staggered: he asked the interpreter to check once again if the minister was really suggesting a change in the constitution. And after the interpreter's confirmation, he said, "Do not translate this, but there is one verse in the Bible I do not think makes much sense. Can he have that changed as well?"

In the past Georgians would consider it inappropriate even to issue invoices. Rather than signing a piece of paper, a Georgian man would say, "I give you my word and a hair from my moustache." A man's promise was more binding than any written proof. Modern Georgians sign legal documents and do not pull out their facial hair to show they are being serious. But the attitude toward contracts is still the same. Most people regard a contract as a formality, something that can be adapted to changed circumstances. What matters is relationships, so if friendships change then contracts can change. Sometimes disagreements are settled in court but most people try to avoid them, as faith and honor are still more important than any legal document.

MANAGING DISAGREEMENT

If you want to avoid disagreements in Georgia it is very important to keep monitoring the situation and to keep in constant touch with your counterparts. Frequent human contact will help preempt most problems. People believe that good relationships are even more important when things do not work.

However, if you still end up in conflict with an individual or a company, it is better to exhaust all possible alternatives before going to court. This might be easier than it sounds. As we have seen, people are only ever one handshake (a degree of separation) away from each other and it is never difficult to find a mediator who will resolve the issue at a lunch or dinner table rather than in the office environment. If the worse comes to the worst and a business relationship breaks down over noncompliance with the terms of a contract, Georgia is subject to the jurisdiction of the European Court of Human Rights. So you can rely on their reputation in adjudicating cases in relation to the violation of property rights.

PEOPLE MANAGEMENT

Georgians often jokingly quote this popular Western business mantra:

Rule 1: The Boss is always right.

Rule 2: If you think the Boss is wrong, refer to Rule 1.

The logic of these rules might seem to apply to the Georgians: people respect authority and are not unreasonably confrontational. Performance is always better, though, when Georgians are motivated by a common goal rather than managed by strict discipline. It's worth keeping in mind that the Georgians are very competitive; they like playing team sports and gambling; they are charismatic and devoted. These qualities make them ideal for a competitive business environment. So it's possible to find a better mantra than "The Boss is the Boss."

chapter nine

COMMUNICATING

THE LANGUAGE

Georgian is a Kartvelian (South Caucasian) language, a group with no apparent relation to any other language family in the world. Its original, distinctive alphabet may be derived from Aramaic with Greek influences—the literary language of pagan Georgia was Aramaic—and the oldest literary Georgian texts date from the fifth century CE.

The British diplomat and traveler Sir John Oliver Wardrop wrote *The Kingdom of Georgia* in 1887. After the First World War he became ambassador to the newly independent state, arriving in 1919 with his sister, Marjory, who was the translator of many Georgian poems, including Rustaveli's *The Knight in the Panther's Skin*. Wardrop remarked upon the way in which the Georgian language resonates with historical meaning.

RESONANT GREETINGS

"As we picked our way among the stones we met many a courteous gentleman . . . . Each raised his tall *papahh* of Astrakhan fur, and, with graceful bow, saluted us, after the manner of the country, with the word *Gamardjweba*, which is, being interpreted, 'I wish thee the victory,' to which we answered *Gaguimardjos* — 'May God grant thee the victory.' These salutations are as eloquent as a dozen volumes of history. I never heard them without thinking of the sad but glorious past of the Georgian kingdom, nobly holding its own, unaided, and witnessing for Christ and His Cross against all the hosts of Islam, performing prodigies of valour that would have added to the fame of Greece or Rome. God grant thee the victory, brave Georgia!"

Modern Georgians still say *Gamargoba* and *Gagimarjos* or *Gaumarjos* when they greet each other. Thousands of years of wars and conquests have marked the Georgian psyche. To wish someone *Gamarjveba* or "victory" is as natural as saying, "Wish you peace this morning" instead of mere "Good morning."

The Georgian language is rich in loan words and phrases that reflect the impact of foreign powers. Christianity brought Greco-Roman influences to Georgia, while the Silk Road imported flavors, goods, and culture from the Middle East and Asia. History speaks though certain words and phrases in the modern language.

Words That Tell Stories

The Georgian word სკოლა (school, pronounced "skola") sounds like the Latin *schola*. The Georgian word ლექსიკონი (vocabulary) is pronounced "leksikoni," like the Greek λεξικό.

From their sound, it seems that certain words, such as შაქარი ("shakari," sugar), მაისური ("maisuri," T-shirt), and აბრეშუმი ("abreshumi," silk) are of Hindi origin.

For centuries the Arabic words for "fate" and "face" have been used as slang, along with Georgian synonyms: ყისმათი ("kissmati"), and სიფათი ("sipati").

There are numerous words that sound like their Turkish equivalents. For example, the word for hammer is pronounced "chakoochi," ჩაქუჩი in Georgian, and as "chaquch," *çekiç* in Turkish.

Obviously, the spoken language bears strong influences of Russian and English.

Georgian Versus Russian

Every single Georgian who has dealt with foreigners has had this conversation at least once:
"Does Georgian sound like Russian?"
"No."
"Do you understand Russian?"
"Yes, but only because I learned it at school. Georgian is absolutely different and it has its own script."
"Do Georgians use Cyrillic?"
"We don't, we use a Georgian alphabet—one of the world's fourteen alphabets. It does not look like Cyrillic or Latin."
"Who else uses the same alphabet?"
"No one else, just Georgians."

The Alphabet

The Georgian Asomtavruli alphabet, invented in the fifth century CE, was gradually replaced by a more angular script in the Middle Ages. In the thirteenth century, the current Mkhedruli alphabet was developed and has been used ever since.

There are thirty-three letters in the modern Georgian alphabet. Each corresponds to a sound, so there are no diphthongs and each letter is always read in one way. This makes it very easy to read and write, but as the grammar is very difficult Georgian is not an easy language to learn.

THE GEORGIAN ALPHABET

ა ani [a]	კ k'ani [k']	ტ t'ani [t']	ძ dzili [dz]
ბ bani [b]	ლ lazi [l]	უ uni [u]	წ ts'ili [ts']
გ gani [g]	მ mani [m]	ფ pari [p]	ჭ ch'ari [č']
დ doni [d]	ნ nari [n]	კ kani [k]	ხ xani [x]
ე eni [e]	ო oni [o]	ღ ghani [y]	ჯ jani [j]
ვ vini [v]	პ p'ari [p']	ყ q'ari [q']	ჰ hae [h]
ზ zeni [z]	ჟ zani [ž]	შ shini [š]	
თ tani [t]	რ rae [r]	ჩ chini [č]	
ი ini [i]	ს sani [s]	ც tsani [ts]	

SPEAKING ENGLISH

The majority of the older generation who were brought up behind the Iron Curtain speak only Russian. Since the collapse of the Soviet Union, however, English has gradually replaced Russian as the most commonly used foreign language. So you will find that most young people speak English, in both cities and rural areas.

JUST BEAR IN MIND

Georgian does not distinguish between "she" and "he," which is why Georgians often make mistakes while using genders in foreign languages.

There are no articles ("a", "the") in Georgian and Georgians keep omitting them in English. The Georgian word for "please" is very old-fashioned and not used in everyday speech, and as a result Georgians can sound very demanding and brusque in English. Do not be surprised if your friend nicely offers you more food by saying, "Take salad!"

Georgian is famous for its consonants. So that it sounds better, "-i" or "-a" are added to every word that finishes on a consonant. The same is done with foreign names. People might refer to you as Beni, rather than Ben.

There are no capital letters in Georgian. Georgians find it hard to grasp the concept of spelling; in their language one letter always corresponds to one sound. So Geoffrey would be just ჯ-ე-ლ-რ-ი (five letters instead of seven).

One letter is always read in one way in Georgian. And even though they have some unpronounceable consonants, for vowels there is only one "i" and one "a" in their alphabet. This makes it almost impossible to hear the difference between "ship" and "sheep" or "crash" and "crush."

And one last thing, just so that you know: in Georgian *deda* is mother and *mama* is father.

THE MEDIA

There are 140 media organizations registered in the country. Half of them are based in Tbilisi, while others cover the whole of Georgia or some of its nine regions.

Studies show that the rural population is more trusting of the media than the urban, and therefore more susceptible to bias and less well informed about the political situation. As rural people have access to only a limited number of TV channels, the ruling party is more popular outside the capital than in Tbilisi. Although Saakashvili's government implemented speedy reforms and changed the country greatly after the Rose Revolution in 2003, contributing to political pluralism and media freedom was at the bottom of their agenda.

TV and Radio

Rustavi 2, which made its reputation for being extremely critical of Eduard Shevardnadze's government, is the most popular independent TV station. The channel was seen as one of the key powers behind the Rose Revolution that brought Mikhail Saakashvili into power. Shortly after 2004, though, the channel's owners changed several times and Rustavi 2 gradually turned into a government mouthpiece. Two other independent channels followed suit: the privately owned Mze and Imedi TV, both critical of Saakashvili, came under heavy pressure from the ruling party. Several years ago the channels' owners changed, and their editorial policy became very similar to that of Rustavi 2. A contemporary cartoon shows hosts of the three national broadcasters as part of the one propaganda machine.

Today most media outlets are divided into pro-government and pro-opposition camps, with the only difference that the pro-opposition channels are small cable-TV outfits with a limited area of coverage, restricted mainly to the capital. The bad news is that the public broadcasters are far from balanced.

So even though Georgian audiences can access many media outlets, they do not receive diverse and comprehensive coverage of news and current affairs from one source.

Two, out of forty regional, national, and cable-TV channels, broadcast in Russian. And out of the same number of radio stations, one has Russian output, while the other, Radio GIPA, rebroadcasts the BBC World Service in English along with its own output.

The Press

The biggest newspapers are private dailies, *24 Saati* (*24 Hours*) and *Rezonansi* (*Resonance*), as well as the weekly *Kvilis Palitra* (*Weekly Palette*). It is also possible to find English newspapers in Tbilisi; ask for the *Financial*, *The Georgian Times*, *Georgia Today*, *The Georgian Journal*, or *The Messenger* if you want to read the local news in English.

SERVICES
Mail
Most Georgians stopped using the national postal service after the collapse of the USSR. The crisis in the 1990s meant that letters took ages to reach their destinations. So ordinary people tend not to post old-fashioned letters and almost no one has their papers delivered to their doorstep. Only big companies subscribe to the newspapers; most people just buy them in kiosks or over the counter in corner shops.

Telephone
Do not expect to find phone booths in Georgia. The safest thing would be to acquire a local SIM card as soon as you arrive. If you have to make an urgent call, ask any stranger in the street or go into the first shop. People are very helpful. Keep in mind, however, that you do need to have ID on you in order to top up your SIM card or to exchange foreign currency.

To call Georgia from abroad dial 00995 5 for cell phones and 00995 32 for landlines. In the past Tbilisi landlines had six digits; recently, however, the number 2 was added at the beginning, so every landline number should have seven digits starting with 2. To make phone calls from Georgia, simply dial 8 and after the tone 00+ (the international number), followed by the country code.

Some Georgians (especially VIPs) do not answer phone calls from unknown or withheld numbers. So it might be better to text rather than call. Keep in mind that texting works better than voice mail: many people just ignore voice messages.

There is a lot of competition in the cell phone market, so there are plenty of cheap offers and deals to choose from. Some Georgians speak for hours with their friends. However, if your Georgian mate suddenly sounds brisk and monosyllabic over the phone, this is because he thinks the conversation might be bugged. This fear is not always groundless, so people prefer to talk in person or on Skype if they want to discuss sensitive issues.

The Internet

The new technologies have brought Georgia closer to the outside world than ever before. Internet penetration is 60 to 70 percent in the capital and major cities, though in rural areas it still is 20 to 30 percent. The number of users is increasing dramatically. According to World Bank data, in 2000 less than 1 percent of the population used the Internet.

Most offices have broadband, but if you need a quick and cheap connection, you can always use dial-up from your cell phone. Ask for available offers in the office of the provider. If you plan to travel in the regions, it's worth checking the coverage in that area. Internet or cell phone providers might tell you that they have the best coverage in all of Georgia, but it's not always true. Different companies have stronger signals in different areas and it's safer to check with someone less biased than your dealer.

There are three main mobile service providers in Georgia—Magti, Geocell, and Beeline. If you want to surf with your smart phone, you will have to go to the office of one of the providers as the service is not enabled by default. For broadband or dial-up Internet you will have to visit the offices of Caucasus Network, Georgia Online, or Sanet. As the rates and offers keep changing, it's worth talking to the operators directly.

CONCLUSION

Today Georgia's strategic geopolitical role is as important as ever, and the cultural legacy of its position at the crossroads of civilizations is evident in its psychological makeup. The Georgian people are a paradoxical mix of their Arab, Persian, and Ottoman conquerors; the Silk Road brought Asian goods to Georgia; and Christianity linked it strongly with the Greco-Roman world. Superimposed upon these layers of ancient history and culture are the seventy-year-old Soviet legacy and a very strong modern Western influence.

To understand the nature of Georgian society you need to consider how historical events, foreign influences, and internal diversity have combined to create something like a beautiful carpet, with many colors and patterns woven into a single intricate image. Whether you can manage only a quick glance, or have the time to study each pattern separately, you could be on the verge of a life-changing experience.

What awaits you in Georgia is its exceptional physical beauty and a passionate people for whom hospitality is a religion. They will welcome you to their generous tables. They will proudly show you their cultural heritage, their haunting folk songs and hymns, dances, and customs. They will demonstrate their readiness to embrace you. And you will not regret it if you open your heart in response.

Further Reading

Anderson, Tony. *Bread and Ashes: A Walk through the Mountains of Georgia*. London: Jonathan Cape, 2003.

De Waal, Thomas. *The Caucasus: An Introduction*. Oxford: OUP, 2010.

Nasmyth, Peter. *Georgia: A Land, its People and Spirit*. London: Stacey International, forthcoming.

———. *Georgia: In the Mountains of Poetry*. Abingdon, UK: Routledge, 2006.

———. *Walking in the Caucasus: Georgia*. London: MTA Publications, 2006.

Parsons, Robert. Chapter in *From Our Own Correspondent: A Celebration of Fifty Years of the BBC Radio Programme* (ed. Tony Grant). London: Profile Books, 2005.

Rayfield, Donald. *Edge of Empires: A History of Georgia*. London: Reaktion Books, 2012.

———. *The Literature of Georgia: A History* (Caucasus World). London: Garnett Press, 2009.

Said, Kurban. *Ali and Nino: A Love Story*. London: Vintage, 2000.

Sebag Montefiore, Simon. *Young Stalin*. London: Phoenix, 2008.

Steavenson, Wendell. *Stories I Stole from Georgia*. London: Atlantic Books, 2002.

Wardrop, Oliver. *Kingdom of Georgia—Notes of Travel in a Land of Women, Wine and Song to which are appended historical literary and political sketches, specimens of the national music and a compendious bibliography*. London: Sampson Low, Marston, Searle, & Rivington, 1888.

Films/Videos

5 Days of War. Action film, also known as *5 Days of August*, depicts 2008 Russian–Georgian War.

English Teacher. Documentary by Nino Orjonikidze and Vano Arsenishvili follows a foreign teacher on his extraordinary visit to Georgia. Watch on www.artefact.ge

Since Otar Left. By Elithabeth Bojan, a film about the resilience of the Georgians during 1990s hardships.

Tell My Friends I'm Dead. Documentary film, by Nino Kirtadze, set in Samegrelo, west Georgia. Extraordinary insight into mourning traditions in Georgia.

That Crazy French Woman in Georgia. Isabelle Legeron takes you to Georgia's aromatic vineyards. http://www.thatcrazyfrenchwoman.com/

Index

Acknowledgments and Dedication

While writing this book I often thought about my childhood and my family. I would like to dedicate this book to them. To my mother who brought me up with regimental discipline and the belief that everything Georgian was special. To my father, a dreamer and a wanderer, who encouraged me to explore the world outside my home country. To my aunt Nellie, I do not have any words to describe how much affection and care she has given me throughout my childhood and how I worship her. And to my uncle Konstantin, who always said that he would learn English if I wrote a book.

Special thanks to all the people who helped with their feedback and advice. I am most grateful to my BBC colleagues from the College of Journalism. And the two people who make everything possible: my daughter Anamaria Burduli and my fiancé Irakli Imnaishvili.